BRENDAN
LIEW

東京

TOKYO

UP LATE

Smith
Street
Books

*Iconic recipes
from the city that
never sleeps.*

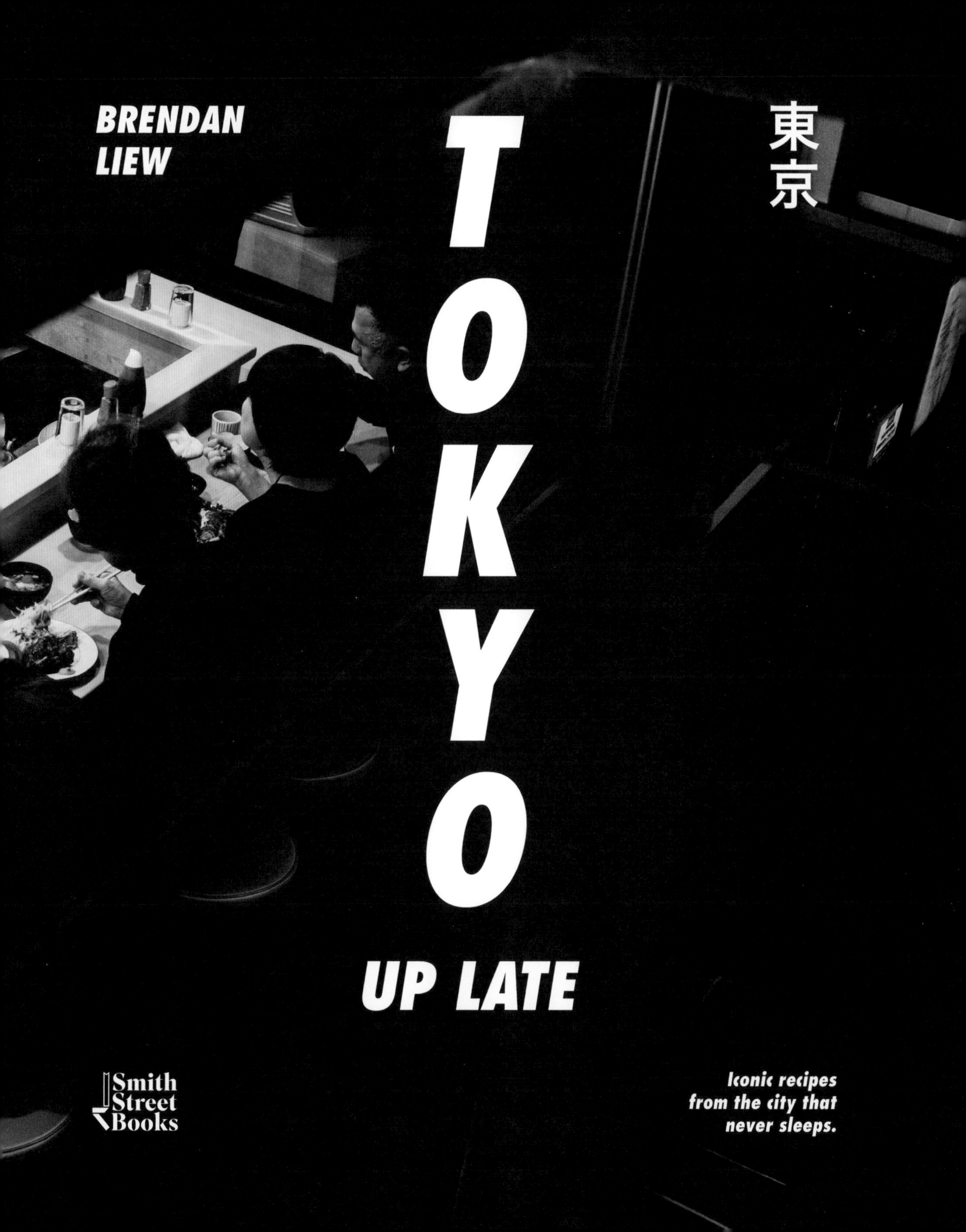

BRENDAN LIEW

東京

TOKYO

UP LATE

Smith Street Books

*Iconic recipes
from the city that
never sleeps.*

Forget your troubles
One cup of cloudy sake
Is all you need

Ōtomo no Tabito,
Collection of Ten Thousand Leaves, 759 AD

験なきものを思はずは
一杯の濁れる酒を
飲むべくあるらし
- 大伴旅人, 万葉集

This book is dedicated to all the late-night restaurant and bar workers in Japan and around the world, and their long-suffering partners who spend countless nights alone. These people strive tirelessly to nourish and offer hospitality to the weary, the drunk and the derelict. Work such as this goes largely unappreciated, but when the night is cold and bleak, and yours is the only welcoming light in the darkness, people are always thankful you're there.

CONTENTS

コンテンツ

NIGHTSCAPE

夜景 YAKEI

The sun has long since disappeared beyond the horizon. In the distance, a bead of light circles Tokyo Skytree, representing the passing of time. Ticking down the seconds until the millions of Tokyo-ites descend onto the city streets, and the rabbit warren of back lanes and alleys light up with the promise of grilled meat, hot noodles and plentiful beer. ◕▶◀ While the daylight shines on the Tokyo of the past, with its beautiful manicured gardens, temples and tea ceremonies, at night is when you see the Tokyo of today. When the people who make up this vast metropolis are free to relax. When the office workers and sales clerks, the waiters and waitresses, the chefs, bar hosts and hostesses clock off, loosen their ties, and let formality slip just a little. The chance to unwind means many different things in the city of Tokyo, with an unrivalled gamut of options available to those seeking sustenance before the long train ride home. ▶◀◕ Izakayas fire up their grills, and the area fills with the aroma of meat searing over hot coals. There's revelry in the air as salarymen and women give in to the tongue-loosening effects of alcohol, cheering trivial joys while congregating over an array of tare-glazed chicken skewers, fresh sashimi and long-stewed miso beef. Another table crowds over a tabletop brazier, searing butter-soft Miyazaki wagyu before quenching it briefly in a salty, garlicky sesame oil, then devouring it between gulps of whisky highballs and refreshing mouthfuls of cool namul. Behind them, the store's touts frantically attempt to charm the last few passers-by before the lanterns extinguish for the night. ◕▶◀ As the evening wears on and the salarymen numbers dwindle in hopes of chasing the last train home, the cooks and waiters sit down and have their own nightly celebration. They drain the rest of the keg and feast on what remains from the day. Stir-fried meat and vegetables in a silky dashi-based ankake sauce, braises of fish collars, crisp croquettes and freshly steamed white rice. Always rice, tonight covered in an array of fresh fish, looking like a jewel box of ocean

treasures, with ruby-like cubes of tuna glistening in the fluorescent izakaya light. Other nights, the rice may be under a blanket of stewed wagyu or a mountain of cabbage, mayonnaise and golden fried fish karaage. ▶◀● In a separate part of the city, the night owls are winding down over a steaming bowl of noodles. The sounds of conviviality from earlier have changed into almost meditative noises. Listening to the rhythmic sound of metal on wood as the udon chef methodically cuts perfect strands of udon noodles, giving full attention to his work even as the clock approaches midnight, the knife strokes as steady as a metronome. Then comes the gentle swishing of noodles in the hot water, followed by a quick thwack as the noodles slam against the side of the basket to liberate them of excess water, which subsequently showers the ground and the udon chef's long gum boots – a melody repeated hundreds of times throughout the evening, millions of times around the city. Always backed by the track of slurping noodles and the rattle of coins being expelled by the vending machine. ●▶◀ As late night turns to early morning, the only lights that remain on are the convenience store's dazzling 750 lux – a beacon of salvation when all other doors are closed, the clerk's unflappable smile almost as luminous as the store's stark white interior. In Japan, going into a convenience store doesn't mean leaving with a hot dog that's been slowly petrifying under greasy heat lamps, or a burrito that has melted into an oily, soggy mess. In Japan it means stepping into a world of gourmet delights, like a wall of 15 varieties of onigiri with fillings such as succulent soy-braised pork or chicken, carefully sourced kombu and sake-marinated salmon roe. Or a suite of sandwiches that may be stuffed with katsu pork, teriyaki chicken, layers of ham and egg, or even fruit and cream. And that's only part of the many temptations that await the late-night gourmet. We haven't even gotten to the fried chicken yet. ▶◀● Past 1 a.m., some tired, hungry souls are just staggering through their front door. They crave something fast and tasty, but healthy enough not to regret the next day – like a warming ochazuke of juicy salmon or cleansing sea bream, a quick bowl of natto (fermented soy beans) with handfuls of vegetables to cleanse

away the excesses, or the late-night classic – instant noodles, dressed up, made nice but still ready in under 10 minutes. ●)(This book celebrates food from the places that welcome Tokyo's citizens who work and party late into the night. These are dishes that work at any time, not just after bedtime. And just as they bring joy and comfort to millions of Tokyo-ites every night, I hope they bring joy and comfort to you, too.

A JAPANESE PANTRY

日本のパントリー NIHON NO PANTORI

Here's a quick guide to stocking your Japanese pantry, from beginner level to more advanced.

ESSENTIAL 必需品 HITSUJUHIN

Below are the basic tools to get you started. Most of the recipes in this book can be made using only these ingredients.

●)◀ *DASHI* (出汁)

The primary cooking liquid in Japanese cuisine is a blend of steeped kombu seaweed and shaved preserved fish, usually bonito, although tuna and mackerel are also common. To make your own, see the dashi recipes in chapter 1 (page 32).

●)◀ *MIRIN* (みりん)

A type of rice wine made from glutinous rice, used to add sweetness and umami to dishes. Real mirin or hon mirin should contain no added sugar, with the sweetness coming from the natural fermentation of glutinous rice with a koji culture.

●)◀ *RICE* (米)

Every grain of rice is valuable: that's the simple adage taught to every Japanese person from a very young age. There are many different types of rice, with varying grades of stickiness, depending on whether it is table rice or sushi rice. Ask your grocer which rice is best for your purpose; rice from Niigata, Aomori, Akita or Hokkaido are good options.

●)◀ *SAKE* (酒 *OR* 料理酒)

An alcohol made from rice, sake can add a floral and light flavour to dishes. For cooking, use only cooking sake, or ryorishu. It has a simple, rounded flavour that pairs well with all food. Drinking sake can have unique flavours and characteristics that may not work well in cooking.

●)◀ *SOY SAUCE* (醤油)

The process of slowly fermenting soy beans, wheat and *Aspergillus oryzae*, a special mould, produces a umami-packed liquid that is the base flavour for many Japanese dishes. There are three main types of soy sauce in Japan:

· usukuchi shoyu (薄口醤油) – light colour, saltiest
· koikuchi shoyu (濃口醤油) – dark colour, medium saltiness
· tamari (たまり) – dark colour, sweet

For all the recipes listed as using soy sauce, we use koikuchi, or dark soy sauce, as it has the most balanced flavour and saltiness. You can also find low-sodium koikuchi shoyu and gluten-free versions. Both these options are fine and will not significantly affect the end result of the dishes.

INTERMEDIATE 中級 CHŪKYŪ

These ingredients will take your Japanese cooking up a level. Many have flavours unique to Japan, but are also popular outside the country, such as miso.

●▶◀ KATSUOBUSHI (BONITO FLAKES) (鰹節)

Katsuobushi is a seasoning made from fillets of bonito (also known as skipjack tuna) that are subjected to a long smoking and drying process, which results in wood-like sticks that are then thinly shaved and used in dashi. There they impart a smoky, savoury flavour that is the base for most traditional Japanese cookery.

●▶◀ KOMBU (昆布)

Dried sheets of kelp with a strong savoury flavour, kombu is the other main ingredient in dashi. It can also be used to cure raw fish and seafood, by sandwiching the ingredient between two sheets of kombu, then leaving it to marinate for anywhere between 10 minutes for thin fish slices, and up to 1 day for whole fish fillets.

●▶◀ NORI (のり/海苔)

These dried seaweed sheets are commonly used to wrap sushi and onigiri. Good-quality nori is crisp, not chewy. It's delicious as a topping for ramen, as it soaks up the ramen broth wonderfully, and is a great snack on its own. Most supermarkets now stock seaweed sheets; if not, check the snack aisle. These seaweeds are usually quite salty, so be careful.

●▶◀ PONZU (ポン酢)

A soy sauce blended with citrus and sometimes bonito flakes, left to infuse for a few days or months. It is used as a dipping sauce for oily fish, such as bonito or mackerel, as a dressing for a beef or tuna tataki, or as a simple salad dressing when mixed with a little oil.

●▶◀ POTATO STARCH (片栗粉)

In the Japanese kitchen, potato starch is a general-purpose thickener of sauces and liquids, mixed with a little water and slowly poured into the boiling liquid. It is also used to coat karaage for that unique, crunchy exterior. You can substitute with cornflour (cornstarch) for thickening, or tapioca starch for deep-frying.

●◐◖ *RICE VINEGAR (酢)*

This vinegar has a mild sourness and sweetness that works in any Japanese salad dressing, and as a vinegar base for pickling. It is much less astringent than Western vinegar, so substitute with caution.

●◐◖ *ROASTED SESAME SEED OIL (ごま油)*

This adds a pleasant nutty characteristic to many dishes, and comes in a variety of grades, from cheap to expensive. The inexpensive versions are fine, but the higher-quality ones will add an extra dimension to your cooking.

●◐◖ *SAIKYO MISO (西京味噌)*

A miso paste that is native to Kyoto, and sweeter than shiro or aka miso paste. It has a creamy texture and colour, and is made with a larger proportion of rice koji than other misos.

●◐◖ *SESAME SEEDS, GRATED (すりごま)*

Sesame seeds are grated in Japan using a suribachi (a traditional Japanese grooved mortar and pestle), or a modern hand-held sesame mill. Both of these result in sesame seeds that are lightly crushed to better release their essential oils. You can do this with a regular mortar and pestle by gently crushing the seeds, or in a spice grinder by pulsing once or twice, being careful not to over-blend and turn them into a paste or powder.

●◐◖ *SESAME SEEDS, ROASTED (胡麻)*

Used either whole or crushed, roasted sesame seeds are a wonderful way to add texture to sashimi, rice and salads. They can also come in a variety of flavours such as ume (pickled plum) or wasabi.

●◐◖ *SHICHIMI TOGARASHI (七味唐辛子)*

A chilli powder made up of seven ingredients is Japan's go-to spice. Shichimi usually contains a combination of ground chilli, sansho pepper, orange peel, black and white sesame seeds, hemp seeds, ginger, nori and poppy seeds. Also available is ichimi, or single spice, which is only chilli flakes.

●◐◖ *SHIRO MISO AND AKA MISO (白味噌 AND 赤味噌)*

Shiro (white) and aka (red) miso paste are the main flavourings for miso soup and a variety of marinated meats, fish and stews. They have a complex sweet, salty flavour that is not possible to substitute. Both misos are made from fermenting soy beans with a koji culture. The difference is that aka miso is fermented longer, and thus has a stronger, saltier flavour, whereas shiro miso can be quite sweet.

●)|(*TEMPURA FLOUR* (天ぷら粉)

Tempura flour creates that light, crisp coating that separates tempura from other fried foods. It is commonly a combination of wheat flour, various starches and baking powder. You can make your own by mixing 300 g (10½ oz) cake flour, 100 g (3½ oz) potato starch or cornflour (cornstarch) and 1 teaspoon baking powder.

●)|(*USUKUCHI SOY SAUCE* (薄口醤油)

See the soy sauce entry on page 15. Use this variety when you want to keep broths and sauces clear in colour, while still providing soy flavour. Usukuchi is widely used in high-end restaurants to make clear soups with great depth.

●)|(*WASABI* (わさび)

Japan may not have many famous spices, and it may not use a lot of chilli, but it does have wasabi with its unique tear-inducing, nose-clearing properties. It is worth seeking out fresh wasabi, but powdered or paste wasabi are suitable substitutes.

●)|(*YUZU KOSHO* (柚子こしょう)

Yuzu citrus rind, chilli and salt left to mature results in a spicy, citrussy condiment that's great with grilled meat and fish or gyoza. Have some on hand at all times for a quick, easy chilli hit.

ADVANCED 上級 JYOUKYŪ

Some of these ingredients can be omitted or substituted. Many have a particular flavour that separates a dish from tasting Japanese-ish to feeling like you're in Japan.

●▷◁ CHICKEN STOCK POWDER (鳥だしの素)

The distinctive flavour in many Chinese–Japanese dishes comes from Chinese or Japanese chicken stock powder. You can omit this ingredient, but some characteristics will be lost. You can substitute with hondashi powder.

●▷◁ KUROZATO / BLACK SUGAR (黒砂糖)

An unrefined black sugar from southern Japan, typically Okinawa. It has a molasses-like taste, and is usually sold in large crystals. It is mainly used in traditional Japanese sweets and desserts such as zenzai, but can be used in stews and braises in place of sugar for a more complex flavour. Substitutes are molasses, dark brown sugar or dark muscovado sugar.

●▷◁ MENTAIKO (明太子)

The salted, preserved roe of the Alaskan pollock fish. Usually found frozen outside of Japan, mentaiko has a clean, briny fish flavour with the added kick of chilli. Tarako (鱈子) is the non-spicy version.

●▷◁ SANSHO (山椒)

Similar to sichuan peppercorns, sansho pepper (usually sold in powdered form) is a citrussy, tongue-numbing spice that is often used in beef cookery. Substitute with shichimi togarashi if unavailable.

●▷◁ SHIO KOMBU (塩昆布)

Strands of dried, salted kombu are wonderful mixed through rice, or chopped and used to garnish salads. They add pleasantly salty oceanic pops of flavour to any application.

●▷◁ SUDACHI, WHOLE OR JUICE (すだち)

A type of Japanese citrus, usually picked green, with very mild sourness, but very savoury. Usually used in broths and meat dishes.

●▶◀ *TAKANA, PICKLED MUSTARD GREENS* (高菜)

A type of salt-preserved green leafy vegetable. It can be used as a topping for ramen, ochazuke, in onigiri, or mixed through fried rice. Chopped Chinese mustard greens are a suitable substitute.

●▶◀ *UMEBOSHI* (梅干し)

Pickled Japanese plums/apricots can add a wonderful fruity sweetness and acidity to dishes, and are great mashed into a salad dressing. Umeboshi is also commonly eaten on its own in the centre of a bowl of rice as a simple meal.

●▶◀ *YUZU, WHOLE OR JUICE* (柚子)

A distinctive Japanese citrus, the flavour of yuzu is impossible to imitate. Used primarily for salad dressings and marinades, it can also add freshness to broths. Substitute with Meyer lemon if unavailable, although the dish won't taste the same.

●▶◀ *ZARAME* (ザラメ)

A type of light brown sugar with large crystals, zarame has more complexity than regular refined white sugar. It is good with meat dishes. Substitute with a light brown sugar, panela or light muscovado sugar.

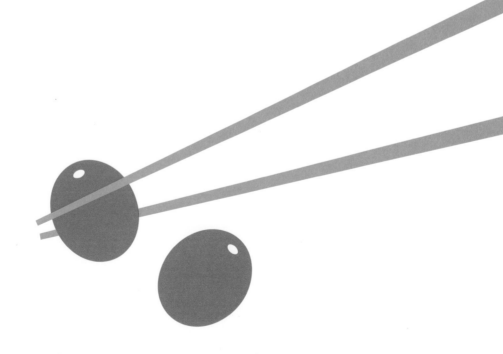

IZAKAYA

居酒屋

NISHI SHINJUKU

Nishi Shinjuku is a modern area, full of hotels and office blocks near Shinjuku station, the busiest train station in the world by passenger number. Hidden away are small pockets such as Omoide Yokocho ('Memory Lane'), a sprawling labyrinth of alleys full of old bars and tiny restaurants that seems totally at odds with the modern buildings looming overhead.

お疲れ様でした

*(Ostukare sama deshita!)**

Beneath the train tracks, it's hard to see where the alley leads. It's so narrow that the store signs can almost touch the ones opposite, like a neon canopy of trees. Beer crates acting as bar stools take up a quarter of the walkway, while lanterns, emblazoned with hiragana spruiking the store's wares, hang at head height to further obstruct the view ahead. People are everywhere – salarymen, teenagers and tourists. The air is thick with the smell of smoke. ●)◀ You and your four colleagues have just finished a big project and are heading to an izakaya to celebrate. You spot one with space and quickly make your way there.

)◀● 何名様ですか? *How many people?* ●)◀ 五名です *Five people, thanks.*

)◀● The matriarch of the izakaya points at five seats on the opposite side of the U-shaped counter. You squeeze your way through, behind the occupied stools, issuing a *sumimasen* (excuse me) as you squeeze past, and take a seat. At the other end of the bar, salarymen, easily identifiable by their dark suits and white shirts, are talking loudly, collars undone, ties hanging loosely around their necks. They hoist their oversized beer mugs and yell *kanpai* (cheers!) before chugging them down, their faces more lobster-red by the second. ●)◀ Beside them, a tourist couple look nervously at each other, trying to decipher the handwritten menu, hoping that if they use one of their few Japanese phrases – *omakase* (leave it to you) – they'll avoid chicken sashimi and shiokara (squid guts).)◀● Ahead, flames shoot out of the grill as a particularly fatty piece of chicken renders golden oil onto the hot coals below. An enormous cauldron sits bubbling alongside. Inside is a dark, rippling mass that could only be motsunabe (intestine stew) – that delectable mess of miso and long-cooked organ meat that melts in the mouth with the slightest pressure of your tongue. Looking around at the staff, you notice there is not a wasted gesture or a moment of hesitation; everything is like clockwork. A perfectly choreographed dance. The customers are jovial with satisfied looks on their faces. You know you made the right choice coming here. ●)◀ Your colleagues next to you are busy debating whether tuna tataki or yukke will make the more appropriate starter. You raise your hand to enter the conversation and say: 取り合えず。おまかせしよ! *For now, leave it to the chef!*

The first izakaya (居酒屋) were liquor stores that allowed customers to buy and consume liquor on their premises. Food offerings were later added, but the izakaya is first and foremost about the alcohol and providing food that complements and encourages drink. Izakayas can take many forms, from tiny bolt-hole, back-alley counters run by a married couple, to massive beer halls owned by international corporations like Asahi and Suntory. ●)(Unlike many other Japanese restaurants, izakayas are unbound by tradition. You'll find many blending Italian, French or German dishes into their menu. As long as it goes well with beer and a well-made whisky highball, it has a place on an izakaya menu. ●)(The quick procession of small plates (otsumami/sakenosakana) is what makes izakaya dining so fun. Strong, salty flavours dominate, such as tsukune (chicken meatballs), coated in soy tare caramelised over binchotan (white charcoal), or saba no misoni – oily mackerel braised in a deep, umami-rich miso sauce. But you can also get the cleanest-tasting, freshest sashimi, crudo or carpaccio you'll ever have the pleasure of eating (a perfect accompaniment to a junmai daiginjo sake) or an array of crisp salads and vegetable dishes (great for refreshing the palate between drinks and heavier dishes). ●)(When you go to an izakaya, don't be afraid to ask what the person next to you is having. There is no formality at an izakaya. The alcohol lubricates any social interaction, and though the servers and chefs may appear stern, they are easy to engage in conversation and will recommend what they're most proud of that night. So don't be daunted if chicken sashimi or squid guts lands in front of you. Smile, pick up your chopsticks and try it. You might be delighted!

頂きます！ (Itadakimasu!)**

* Japanese phrases such as this don't have an exact equivalent in English. Ostukare sama deshita ('Thank you for your work today') is said amongst employees as they're leaving – like saying 'goodbye' after work.

** Itadakimasu ('Thank you for the food' – but literally, 'I receive') is always said before eating as a thankyou to the person who prepared the meal, but is also said even if the person who prepared the meal isn't there. It is like saying grace to everyone who contributed to the food.

DASHI
出汁 STOCK

An infusion of seaweed and bonito flakes (katsuobushi), dashi is the backbone of Japanese cuisine, full of umami, and the base for carrying flavour in almost all traditional dishes. If you have time, method 1 below is the best way to make it. If you don't have time, almost all Asian grocers have high-quality dashi packs that resemble tea bags (second-best option), or dashi powder (third-best option).

METHOD 1: THE TRADITIONAL WAY, MAKES 2 LITRES (8 CUPS)

2 litres (8 cups) water, at room temperature ▶ filtered 12 g (¼ oz) kombu ▶ 25 g (1 oz) katsuobushi

Pour the water into a large pot, add the kombu and allow to steep for 30 minutes. Place over high heat. When bubbles start rising (at about 70°C/160°F), remove the kombu.

Bring the water to about 80°C (175°F), then add the katsuobushi. Keep the heat on until 85°C (185°F), or when small bubbles are rising, then turn off the heat.

When the katsuobushi sinks to the bottom of the pot, strain through a fine-meshed strainer or muslin (cheesecloth). Do not press the katsuobushi, as it will introduce unwanted flavours; you can use the left-over kombu and katsuobushi to make niban dashi (second dashi) by re-simmering the ingredients in another 2 litres (8 cups) water for 10 minutes, which will make a good base for a stew.

Allow the dashi to cool, then refrigerate for up to 3 days.

METHOD 2: THE QUICK WAY, MAKES 750 ML (3 CUPS)

1 instant dashi tea bag ▶ 750 ml (3 cups) water

Bring the water to a simmer in a small saucepan, then add the dashi tea bag.

Press the tea bag down into the water and simmer for 1 minute.

Turn off the heat and taste the broth. If it's not strong enough, you can leave the dashi bag in for another 1–5 minutes.

When the broth is flavourful, remove the the dashi bag.

If you're not using the dashi immediately, allow the liquid to cool, then store in the fridge. The dashi will keep refrigerated for up to 2 days.

METHOD 3: THE INSTANT WAY, MAKES 750 ML (3 CUPS)

1 tablespoon hon dashi powder ▶ 750 ml (3 cups) boiling water

Whisk together the dashi powder and boiling water.

Taste, then add more water or powder until you have a balanced dashi.

OTOSHI

お通し SMALL BITES

Izakayas will often charge a seating fee and, in exchange for that seating fee, they will give diners an otoshi, or complementary snack. It could be some pickled vegetables, a small karaage, a little sashimi or, in places where the main event is rich – such as a kushikatsu restaurant or yakiniku – it could be some fresh seasonal vegetables with a miso dipping sauce.

SOY BUTTER EDAMAME 醤油バター枝豆
SERVES 2 TO SHARE

1 tablespoon neutral-flavoured oil ▶ 1 garlic clove, crushed ▶ 1 dried chilli, seeds removed, thinly sliced, or ½ teaspoon chilli flakes ▶ 150 g (5½ oz) edamame beans, boiled ▶ 1 teaspoon salt ▶ 1 tablespoon soy sauce ▶ ½ tablespoon butter

Edamame is probably the most famous otoshi and izakaya snack. If you've never eaten edamame before, it seems slightly strange at first to extract the beans using your teeth, while sucking the salt from the exterior of the pod, but once you're used to it, you'll find yourself addicted to the snack and able to finish a whole bowl in an instant. This recipe creates edamame coated in a slightly salty and spicy butter. The butter envelops the beans in the soy, garlic and chilli, to really pack more flavour into each bean.

Heat the oil in a large frying pan over medium–high heat. Add the garlic and chilli and fry for 30 seconds, being careful not to burn the garlic.

Throw in the edamame beans and cook, tossing regularly, for 2–3 minutes, or until they start to brown.

Turn off the heat and mix in the remaining ingredients, coating the beans evenly.

Transfer the beans to a plate, scraping the pan to scoop out all the butter and soy sauce.

Serve with a small empty plate on the side for the empty pods.

VEGETABLE MISO 野菜味噌 *SERVES 2 TO SHARE*

300 g (10½ oz) fresh vegetables such as cabbage, tomato, capsicum (bell pepper), carrot or cucumber ◗ 4 tablespoons shiro miso paste ◗ 2 tablespoons yuzu juice or rice vinegar ◗ 1 tablespoon grated sesame seeds ◗ 1 tablespoon sugar ◗ 1 tablespoon sake ◗ 1 tablespoon soy sauce ◗ 1 garlic clove, grated

This plate of miso and vegetables, usually tomato, spring onion (scallion) and cucumber, but always with a wedge of crisp, sweet cabbage, is a great accompaniment to cleanse the palate after bites of rich, oily meat.

Cut the vegetables into wedges or pieces that are easy to scoop up the miso with.

Mix all the remaining ingredients together and serve as a dip for the fresh vegetables. The mixture can also be used as a dipping sauce for yakiniku (page 68).

MAGURO TATAKI

マグロたたき TUNA TATAKI

A classic izakaya dish, tuna tataki is also a great representation of Japanese cuisine in general – taking a fantastic ingredient at its peak and letting it shine by giving it a simple dressing that accentuates its flavour, and serving it with a small salad to add freshness and create a textural and visual contrast to the ruby-red tuna.

If you can, buy some different parts of the tuna, such as the akami (red meat), chutoro (medium fatty meat) and otoro (fatty meat), to appreciate the different flavours and textures of the tuna.

300 g (10½ oz) tuna

salt, for seasoning

125 ml (½ cup) neutral-flavoured oil

3 garlic cloves, thinly sliced

1 shallot, thinly sliced

2 spring onions (scallions), thinly sliced

10 cm (4 inch) piece of cucumber, julienned

1 bunch of micro greens, or a handful of mizuna

DRESSING

1 tablespoon grated fresh daikon, strained

1 tablespoon grated fresh ginger

1 garlic clove, grated

3 tablespoons soy sauce

1½ tablespoons mirin

1 tablespoon rice vinegar

1 tablespoon sudachi or yuzu juice

SERVES 2 AS A SHARED STARTER

If you have a kitchen blow torch, salt the tuna, then torch it all over. If you don't, heat a frying pan over high heat, coat the tuna in oil, then sprinkle with salt and quickly sear on all sides until each side is coloured.

Place the tuna in the refrigerator to cool; this makes it easier to slice.

While the tuna is cooling, combine all the dressing ingredients and set aside.

In a small saucepan, combine the oil and garlic. Heat over medium heat, stirring occasionally, until the garlic is lightly golden brown. Remove the garlic, allowing it to drain and cool on paper towel. Sprinkle with a little salt.

Take the tuna out of the fridge. Cut into 5 mm (¼ inch) thick slices and arrange on a serving plate.

Mix together the shallot, spring onion, cucumber and greens. Place in the centre of the plate.

Spoon the dressing over, sprinkle with the garlic chips and serve.

TAKO WAFU CARPACCIO

蛸和風カルパッチョ JAPANESE-STYLE OCTOPUS CARPACCIO

Tako wasa, raw octopus marinated in a wasabi dressing, is a popular dish in izakayas and at home. It is so popular that every supermarket and convenience store sells it. The Japanese love the slightly chewy texture of the octopus, mixed with the punchy wasabi. Sometimes chopped fresh wasabi stem is also added for a greater textural contrast.

Many modern izakayas take a little bit of East and West; this dish is a harmonious blend of the Italian carpaccio and the traditional tako wasa.

300 g (10½ oz) octopus tentacles

2 tablespoons + 1 teaspoon salt

1.25 litres (5 cups) dashi (page 32)

3 tablespoons olive oil

1 tablespoon soy sauce

1 tablespoon lemon juice

1 tablespoon finely diced shallot

½ teaspoon grated fresh wasabi

2 shiso leaves or flat-leaf (Italian) parsley sprigs, very finely chopped

¼ teaspoon ground black pepper

¼ teaspoon salt

SERVES 2 AS PART OF A SHARED MEAL

Place the octopus in the sink. Using the 2 tablespoons salt, massage the octopus for 2–3 minutes to remove the slime, then rinse.

Bring 1 litre (4 cups) water to the boil in a saucepan and prepare a bowl of cold water. Dip the octopus into the boiling water for 10 seconds, then immediately place into the cold water. Rinse the octopus in the cold water to get rid of any residual slime and cool the octopus. Drain.

In a saucepan, bring the dashi and 1 teaspoon salt to a simmer, then turn off the heat and place the octopus in. Place a lid on and leave for 20 minutes.

After 20 minutes, place the octopus in a container. Pour the dashi over, then refrigerate until cold, or overnight.

When ready to serve, remove the octopus from the liquid and dry it. Discard the liquid. Thinly slice the octopus and arrange on a serving dish.

Mix together the remaining ingredients and spoon over the octopus.

YUKKE

ユッケ KOREAN-STYLE STEAK OR FISH TARTARE

The Korean dish yukhoe, a kind of steak tartare, has become very popular in izakayas. The strong flavours of gochujang and garlic pair well with alcohol. The Japanese have incorporated their love of seafood into it by replacing the beef of the Korean version with tuna or salmon.

This is a great dish for communal dining, or as a simple one-dish meal on its own when served over hot rice.

200 g (7 oz) tuna, salmon or beef fillet, as fresh as possible from a reputable supplier

2 tablespoons soy sauce

1 tablespoon mirin

1 tablespoon sesame oil

2–3 teaspoons gochujang

½ garlic clove, grated

1 nori sheet

cooked hot rice, to serve (optional)

2 eggs

2 tablespoons toasted sesame seeds

8 shiso leaves, shredded

2 spring onions (scallions), thinly sliced

4 chives, chopped

SERVES 2 AS A RICE DISH, OR 4 AS A SHARED APPETISER

Remove any fat or sinew from your chosen protein. If using beef, dice it into 1 cm (½ inch) cubes. If using fish, dice it into cubes or slice thinly.

In a bowl, mix together the soy sauce, mirin, sesame oil, gochujang and garlic, then add your protein and mix well. Add more soy and gochujang if you desire.

Toast the nori sheet by waving it quickly over your stovetop flame, being very careful not to set it alight. It should turn crisp. Break into small pieces and set aside.

IF MAKING THE YUKKE AS A RICE DISH:

Place the rice in the bottom of two bowls. Place the yukke mixture on top, making an indent in the centre.

Crack an egg into a bowl. Gently scoop the yolk from the white, then place the yolk in the centre of one of the bowls; reserve the egg white for another use. Repeat with the other egg and yukke bowl. Dress with the remaining ingredients.

IF SERVING THE YUKKE AS A SHARED DISH:

Simply divide the yukke between two plates, preferably using a ring mould to keep it round. Place an egg yolk in the centre of each, as above, then arrange the remaining ingredients on top.

FUWAFUWA DASHI MAKI TAMAGO

ふわふわだし巻き卵 FLUFFY JAPANESE ROLLED OMELETTE

Learning the technique to make this fluffy Japanese omelette is so embedded in Japanese schools and culture that, to locals, it's as straightforward as riding a bike. For people who did not grow up with it, the technique, which requires a flick of the wrist and a deft chopstick hand, looks almost impossible to master. Get yourself a non-stick tamago pan (avoid the traditional copper ones unless you're very confident or very patient), a few eggs, a long pair of chopsticks and have a go! Even if your omelette rolling doesn't work the first time, the results will still be delicious.

4 eggs

125 ml (½ cup) dashi

1 teaspoon soy sauce

2 teaspoons mirin

a pinch of salt

1 teaspoon potato starch

2 tablespoons neutral-flavoured oil

TO SERVE

1 tablespoon grated fresh daikon

1 tablespoon soy sauce

SERVES 2–3 AS PART OF A SHARED MEAL

Whisk together the eggs, dashi, soy sauce, mirin and salt.

Place the potato starch in a bowl. Strain about 60 ml (¼ cup) of the egg mixture into the potato starch and whisk until uniform. Strain in the remainder of the egg mixture and whisk until the mixture is smooth and no streaks of egg yolk or white are visible.

Heat a 20 cm (8 inch) tamagoyaki pan over medium heat and add the oil. Swirl the oil around to coat the pan, then pour the oil from the pan into a small bowl and reserve.

Pour one-third of the egg mixture into the pan and swirl to evenly coat the pan. Using chopsticks, puncture any large air bubbles to create a mostly flat surface. When the egg mixture is mostly set (if you pick up the pan and gently swirl it, the egg doesn't flow freely), begin rolling the egg over, starting from the side furthest away from you and rolling towards you. You should have a squarish, Swiss-roll shaped omelette.

Using chopsticks, dip a piece of paper towel into the oil and use that to grease the empty side of the pan. Push the omelette to the side of the pan furthest from you and grease where the omelette previously was.

Pour in another one-third of the egg mixture and swirl it around the pan, lifting the omelette so the raw egg runs underneath and sticks to the omelette; this also prevents the omelette getting too browned on the bottom.

When the egg is mostly set, repeat the rolling process, then complete the omelette with the final one-third of the egg mixture.

Turn the omelette out onto a cutting board. Carefully slice into six pieces and transfer to a serving dish. Serve with daikon drizzled with soy sauce on the side.

HARUSAME SALAD

春雨サラダ GLASS NOODLE SALAD

The Japanese poetically call glass noodles harusame – 'spring rain' – due to their ethereal, translucent appearance, resembling flowing water. There are many uses for glass noodles. One of the most common is in a colourful and invigorating chilled salad with ham and shredded vegetables in a rice vinegar dressing. Refreshing as light rain on a warm spring evening.

½ carrot, peeled and shredded

½ telegraph (long) cucumber, seeds removed, thinly sliced

1 tablespoon salt

120 g (4½ oz) glass noodles; those made from rice or sweet potato are both suitable

100 g (3½ oz) fresh black fungus, or a handful of dried black fungus rehydrated in warm water, shredded

50 g (1¾ oz) ham, thinly sliced

1 sheet of kinshi tamago (page 96), shredded

chilli oil, to serve

roasted sesame seeds, to serve

DRESSING

60 ml (¼ cup) rice vinegar

3 tablespoons soy sauce

3 tablespoons sugar

3 tablespoons roasted sesame oil

1 teaspoon chicken stock powder

SERVES 4 AS PART OF A SHARED MEAL

Place the carrot and cucumber in a colander, add the salt and mix. Leave for 5 minutes to drain, then squeeze out the excess moisture and set aside.

Rehydrate the noodles according to the packet instructions. Drain and rinse under cold water, then drain thoroughly.

In a bowl, mix together the dressing ingredients, then add to the noodles along with carrot, cucumber, black fungus and ham.

Refrigerate for 15 minutes to let the flavours develop.

Mix in the kinshi tamago and place on a serving dish. Drizzle with chilli oil, sprinkle with sesame seeds and serve.

TOFU NO MIZORE

豆腐の霙 SIMMERED TOFU WITH GRATED DAIKON SAUCE

The grated daikon added to this dish is referred to as mizore – ice – *for its resemblance to shaved ice. In Japan, grated daikon is often added to hotpots or nabes, to lend body and texture to the broth. It is most common in winter, to reflect the falling snow outside.*

This is a basic version of tofu no mizore*, to be served as a side dish – but you can scale the liquid and daikon up three or four times, and add various vegetables and thinly sliced meats to create a bountiful hotpot for a satisfying one-dish meal.*

15 cm (6 inch) piece of daikon

100 ml (3½ fl oz) dashi (page 32)

1 tablespoon mentsuyu (page 216)

500 g (1 lb 2 oz) block of deep-fried tofu (atsuage tofu) or momen tofu, cut into 8 pieces

1 spring onion (scallion), thinly sliced

SERVES 4 AS PART OF A SHARED MEAL

Peel and grate the daikon. Place the grated daikon on a sheet of paper towel or a clean tea towel, bring the sides up and gently squeeze the daikon to remove some of the liquid. Set aside.

In a saucepan with a lid, bring the dashi to a simmer over medium heat, then stir in the mentsuyu. Add the tofu, place the lid on and simmer for 2 minutes, then add the daikon and gently stir through.

Cook for a few minutes until the daikon is warm.

Transfer to a serving dish and serve sprinkled with the spring onion.

SALADS
サラダ

Izakaya salads are often presented as the appetiser before the cooked meat and seafood dishes. Therefore, they must be mouthwatering, interesting and delicious in their own right. Below are a few easy, refreshing salads you can use to start your meal.

CUCUMBER TATAKI 胡瓜たたき

2 Lebanese (short) cucumbers

2 teaspoons salt

2 tablespoons shredded fresh ginger

1 tablespoon sesame oil

1 tablespoon soy sauce

1 tablespoon vinegar

½ teaspoon sugar

1 teaspoon mirin

1 dried chilli, seeds removed, thinly sliced

SERVES 2 AS PART OF A SHARED MEAL

Place the cucumbers in a bowl and sprinkle with 1 teaspoon of the salt. Massage the salt into the cucumber skins for 30 seconds, or until liquid starts leaching out of the cucumbers.

Place the cucumbers on a chopping board. Using a rolling pin, gently hit the cucumbers all over to crack them, then slice into bite-sized pieces.

Transfer to a colander over the sink. Work in the remaining 1 teaspoon salt, then leave for 10 minutes. (Salting and gently bashing the cucumbers helps remove the liquid and create more surface area, so the cucumber can absorb the salad dressing.)

Meanwhile, mix together all the remaining ingredients.

Using your hands or a tea towel, squeeze as much liquid from the cucumber as possible. Toss the cucumber through the dressing, then marinate in the refrigerator for 10 minutes.

Transfer to your serving dish, drizzling any excess dressing over.

TOMATO, WAKAME & SHIRASU SALAD トマト、若布、しらすサラダ

2 tablespoons dried wakame

200 g (7 oz) tomatoes

2 tablespoons katsuobushi

1 tablespoon shredded fresh ginger

1 tablespoon shirasu (optional)

1 tablespoon rice vinegar

1 tablespoon olive oil

½ teaspoon sugar

½ teaspoon salt

¼ teaspoon ground black pepper

Put the wakame in a bowl, cover with cold water and set aside for about 10 minutes to rehydrate.

Cut the tomatoes into random, bite-sized pieces. Mix together in a bowl with the remaining ingredients.

Drain the rehydrated wakame and squeeze out the excess moisture. Add to the salad and stir well, then transfer to your serving dish.

SERVES 2 AS PART OF A SHARED MEAL

DAIKON & MENTAI MAYO SALAD 大根、明太、マヨサラダ

300 g (10½ oz) daikon

2 tablespoons mentaiko, plus an extra 1 teaspoon to garnish

1 tablespoon mayonnaise

1 teaspoon rice vinegar

½ teaspoon salt

a handful of spinach or salad greens

1 tablespoon finely sliced chives

2 tablespoons kizami nori (shredded nori)

Peel and julienne the daikon, then submerge in cold water for 10 minutes to make the daikon more crisp.

Drain the daikon and leave in a colander to dry.

In a bowl, mix together the mentaiko, mayonnaise, vinegar and salt, then add the daikon and spinach.

Transfer to a serving dish. Top with the chives, nori and extra mentaiko and serve.

SERVES 2 AS PART OF A SHARED MEAL

SALAD PHOTOGRAPHY OVERLEAF →

TOMATO, WAKAME & SHIRASU SALAD

CUCUMBER TATAKI

DAIKON & MENTAI MAYO SALAD

SABA NO MISONI

鯖の味噌煮 MISO-BRAISED PACIFIC MACKEREL

Mackerel is one of the more polarising fish for people outside Japan. I believe it's mainly because the mackerel they've eaten isn't fresh or is improperly treated. When treated well, its flavour can be sublime, like a taste of the clean ocean when used as sashimi, or succulent and tender when braised, as in this recipe. The sweet miso and spicy ginger pair well with the oily nature of the fish, and the sauce goes great atop a mound of steaming-hot rice.

1 whole mackerel or saba, about 500 g (1 lb 2 oz)

250 ml (1 cup) dashi (page 32)

3 tablespoons shiro miso paste

3 tablespoons sake

1 tablespoon mirin

½ tablespoon sugar

4 cm (1½ inch) piece of fresh ginger

SERVES 3 OR 4 AS PART OF A SHARED MEAL

Fillet the mackerel and remove all the bones (you can ask your fishmonger to do this). Cut the fish into 5 cm (2 inch) wide pieces, discarding the last 2 cm (¾ inch) from the tail; you should have six pieces. Cut a cross in the skin side, at the thickest part, to help the sauce penetrate into the fish.

Bring a kettle of water to the boil. Place the mackerel, skin side up, in a colander, then pour the boiling water over the fish; the skin should visibly contract. Place on a plate while you prepare the braising sauce.

In a saucepan, combine the dashi, miso paste, sake, mirin and sugar. Bring to the boil to dissolve the sugar, mixing well.

Meanwhile, make a cartouche out of baking paper to fit the saucepan. Peel the ginger, then slice it in half. Cut one half into slices, and the other half into julienne strips, keeping them separate. Set aside.

Add the mackerel pieces to the saucepan in one layer. Scatter the ginger slices over. Bring to the boil, then reduce the heat to a simmer. Place the cartouche directly on the mackerel and simmer for 30 minutes over low heat.

Check there is still liquid in the pan, topping up with water if needed, so that the liquid comes about three-quarters of the way up the fish. Simmer for another 10 minutes.

Remove from the heat, then discard the cartouche. Place the fish in your serving dish, drizzle any remaining liquid over and serve garnished with the julienned ginger.

TSUKUNE

つくね

A subset of the yakitori (skewered grilled chicken) restaurant is the tsukune specialist. Tsukune are chicken meatballs, grilled over an open flame, then traditionally dipped into a soy-based sauce, or tare. These tsukune specialist restaurants are not fancy or considered the pinnacle of yakitori cooking. Instead, they are fun establishments where the focus is on the drinks and the proprietor creating tsukune with unique, eye-catching and punchy toppings.

Here you'll find a basic tsukune recipe, along with a few toppings for you to try with it. Have fun with the variations, mixing and matching to find your personal favourite.

TARE タレ

75 ml (2½ fl oz) soy sauce
75 ml (2½ fl oz) mirin
25 ml (¾ fl oz) sake
50 g (1¾ oz) raw sugar
2 spring onion (scallion) tops

MAKES ABOUT 125 ML (½ CUP)

Place all the ingredients in a saucepan, except the spring onion tops. Cook over medium–low heat for about 10–15 minutes, until reduced by one-quarter.

Add the spring onion tops and simmer for another 10 minutes. Strain, discarding the spring onion.

Leave to cool, then store in the refrigerator for up to 1 month.

TSUKUNE つくね

200 g (7 oz) onion

500 g (1 lb 2 oz) minced (ground) chicken (thighs, preferably)

50 g (1¾ oz) chicken cartilage (optional), finely chopped (see note)

1 egg white

50 g (1¾ oz) silken tofu

1 tablespoon salt

1 teaspoon ground black pepper

125 ml (½ cup) tare (optional; see recipe opposite)

MAKES 12 SKEWERS

Bring a pot of water to a simmer.

Very finely chop the onion, then rinse in three changes of cold water. Drain well, then dry on paper towel.

Put the chicken mince in a bowl, with the chicken cartilage, if using. Add the onion, egg white, tofu, salt and pepper, mixing well with your hands. The mixture should feel loose at first, but keep mixing and it will become stickier and easier to form into balls.

Using a teaspoon, take spoonfuls of the mixture and drop them into the simmering water. Poach for 3 minutes, then drain and cool.

Thread three meatballs onto each skewer and refrigerate until ready to cook.

If proceeding with the toppings below, season with salt and barbecue or pan-fry the meatballs with a little oil until cooked, then dress as instructed below.

If using the tare, barbecue or pan-fry the meatballs until browned, brush with the tare and continue to cook until caramelised. Dip again in tare and serve.

NOTE: *Chicken cartilage adds a crunchy, textural contrast to the tsukune. Your butcher will be able to supply you with this.*

TSUKUNE TOPPINGS つくねのトッピング

EACH TOPPING MAKES ENOUGH FOR 2 SKEWERS

Mustard + mayonnaise: Mix together 1 tablespoon mayonnaise and ½ teaspoon Japanese mustard paste.

Yuzu kosho + mayonnaise: Add a dot of yuzu kosho to each meatball, then squiggle some mayonnaise over.

Mentaiko + mayonnaise: Mix 1 tablespoon mentaiko with 1 tablespoon mayonnaise; top with shredded spring onion (scallion) greens.

Wasabi + mayonnaise: Mix together 1 tablespoon mayonnaise and ½ teaspoon wasabi paste; sprinkle with black sesame seeds.

Tsukimi (egg yolk): Cook the meatballs with the tare (see recipe); serve with a raw egg yolk for dipping.

Umeboshi + shiso: Remove the stone from 1 umeboshi and chop the flesh. Top each meatball with a little umeboshi and finish with shredded shiso leaves.

Cheese: Cook the meatballs with the tare (see recipe), then cover each skewer with a slice of cheese. Grill the meatballs using an oven grill (broiler) or kitchen blow torch to melt and brown the cheese.

TSUKUNE PHOTOGRAPHY OVERLEAF →

TSUKUNE

NIKUMAKI

肉巻き PAN-FRIED VEGETABLES WRAPPED IN MEAT

A quick, fun and simple dish of vegetables and cheese rolled in thin slices of meat and covered in sauce, nikumaki is a favourite of housewives and izakayas alike. In summer it is made using the best seasonal tomatoes and zucchini; in winter it is often a melody of mushrooms. It can be made inexpensively using pork belly, or elevated by using wagyu. Either way, the results far exceed the little effort required for this dish.

400 g (14 oz) assorted vegetables such as enoki mushrooms, zucchini (courgettes), asparagus, cherry tomatoes, capsicum (bell pepper), okra

400 g (14 oz) pork belly (skin off) or beef, thinly sliced

salt and black pepper, for seasoning

20 shiso leaves (optional)

50 g (1¾ oz) shredded cheese (optional)

2 tablespoons potato starch

3 tablespoons soy sauce

3 tablespoons mirin

3 tablespoons sake

1 tablespoon sugar

1 teaspoon grated fresh ginger

2 tablespoons neutral-flavoured oil

mayonnaise, to serve

green salad, to serve

SERVES 4

Clean the vegetables and cut into finger-sized pieces.

Lay the pork belly or beef out on a board. Sprinkle with salt and pepper. Place a vegetable piece on one edge, with a shiso leaf and some cheese, if using, then roll up. Repeat with the remaining vegetables and meat.

Dust the rolls with the potato starch.

In a small bowl, mix together the soy sauce, mirin, sake, sugar and ginger.

Heat a large frying pan over medium heat. Add the oil, then place the rolls in the pan, seam side down. Allow to brown for 1–2 minutes, then turn the rolls over.

When browned on the other side, turn the rolls around so that every side is coloured.

Add the soy sauce mixture and allow the sauce to reduce for about 5 minutes, while constantly turning the rolls around in the sauce to coat completely.

Remove from the heat and place on a serving dish, pouring the excess sauce over.

Serve with mayonnaise and a green salad.

YU-AN YAKI

幽庵焼き GRILLED FISH IN YU-AN STYLE MARINADE

A tea ceremony master and gourmet named Kitamura Yu-an (1648–1719) is credited with creating a marinade of soy, sake and mirin that bears his name. He was the first to use mirin in cooking, as it had previously only been consumed as a beverage.

Yu-an yaki is anything grilled that has been steeped in Yu-an's marinade, which is very popular and can be used on almost any meat or fish. Here we are using fish, and cooking it under the oven grill (broiler), but proteins marinated this way can also be barbecued, pan-fried or roasted.

This is a modified version of Yu-an's marinade, with the inclusion of saikyo miso paste and yuzu. The yuzu gives a nice citrus kick, while the miso lends more complexity and sweetness.

4 x 150 g (5½ oz) fish fillets (see note)

125 ml (½ cup) sake

80 ml (⅓ cup) mirin

40 ml (1½ fl oz) soy sauce

80 g (2¾ fl oz) saikyo miso paste

20 ml (¾ fl oz) yuzu juice

½ lemon

SERVES 4

Check the fish fillets and remove any scales and pin bones. You can leave the skin on or take it off, whichever you prefer. Place on paper towel and refrigerate while you prepare the marinade.

In a small saucepan, warm the sake over high heat until it comes to the boil, then continue to boil for 1 minute. Be careful, as the mixture may catch on fire at this stage; you want to cook off some of the alcohol, so this is normal.

Remove from the heat, then mix in the soy sauce and miso paste until there are no lumps. Add the yuzu juice, squeeze in the juice from the lemon and drop the lemon skin in as well. Place in the refrigerator to cool down.

Once cooled, place half the marinade in an airtight container. Add the fish fillets in a single layer, then pour the remaining marinade over. Place a sheet of paper towel directly onto the marinade. (This ensures any bits of fish that aren't adequately covered by the marinade are still marinated through contact with the paper, and also prevents the surface from becoming dryer than anything submerged, which would cause it to burn.) Cover the container and refrigerate overnight.

The next day, gently scrape the marinade off the fish. Bring the fish to room temperature by leaving it out of the fridge for 20 minutes, covered. Discard the marinade.

Preheat your oven grill (broiler). Line a baking tray with foil.

Place the fish on the baking tray, then place on the middle rack of your oven. Grill (broil) gently for about 8–10 minutes, checking regularly so the fish doesn't burn. When the fish looks darkened in spots, test it by pressing gently with chopsticks or kitchen tongs; the fish should flake easily. (Another method is to poke a cake tester into the centre of the fish and leave it there for 5 seconds. Remove and touch your upper lip with the end of the cake tester. If it is hot, the fish is done. If the fish looks done but is still cold inside, place on a lower rack of the oven and continue cooking a little longer.)

When the fish is done, remove from the tray using a spatula and place on serving plates. Wonderful served with rice and miso soup.

NOTE: Choose a fatty fish with thick fillets such as salmon, trout, sea bass or cod. These thick fillets will not over-marinate in the time given, and will be more succulent at the end of the cooking process

KAMO NEGI
鴨ネギ DUCK WITH GRILLED LEEKS

Like bacon and eggs, kamo (duck) and negi (leek) can be listed as just two ingredients on a menu, but the combination is so well known in Japan that people can envisage the dish based only on those two words alone.

Kamo negi is usually seared, thinly sliced duck breast accompanied by the whites of leeks that have been slowly pan-fried or roasted to have nicely brown grill marks. It could be served plated as an okazu (side dish) as part of a larger feast, or made into a delightful noodle soup. I've included both versions of the dish here, as you can double the amount of duck breast and turn it into two completely different meals.

It is best to start this recipe the day before, to allow the duck breast to cure with the salt and sansho overnight. This draws out water from the meat while seasoning the duck at the same time, resulting in crispier duck skin and more flavoursome meat.

2 duck breasts

2 teaspoons salt

1 teaspoon ground sansho pepper

1 thin leek, cleaned, whites cut into 4 pieces, greens discarded or used for stock

30 ml (1 fl oz) soy sauce

30 ml (1 fl oz) sake

15 g (½ oz) zarame or sugar

Using a sharp knife, remove any silver skin from the underside of the duck breasts. Rub 1 teaspoon salt over the skin and meat of each breast, then rub the sansho pepper over only the flesh. (We season only the meat side with the sansho, because the sansho will burn on the skin side, which is pan-fried for a longer time than the meat side.)

Place the duck breasts, skin side up, on a rack with a tray underneath. Leave uncovered in the refrigerator for up to 24 hours, but at least 2 hours.

When ready to cook, use a sharp knife to cut lines down the duck skin, along the length of the breast, about 2 mm (⅛ inch) deep and 1 cm (½ inch) apart. This creates channels for the duck fat to render out, resulting in a crispier skin.

Place the duck, skin side down, in a cold frying pan and turn the heat to medium–low. When the duck starts sizzling and a thin layer of rendered duck fat coats the bottom of the pan, add the leek to the pan.

Cook for 15 minutes over medium–low heat, skin side down the whole time; there should be a light frying noise. Every 5 minutes, drain the fat from the pan, reserving it for roasted potatoes or stir-fries. Turn the leek over after 7 minutes.

Meanwhile, in a small saucepan, heat the soy sauce, sake and zarame just enough to dissolve the zarame.

At this point, you can take the recipe in two different directions.

PLATED VERSION

1 bunch of spring onions
(scallions)

SOUP VERSION

500 ml (2 cups) dashi
(page 32)

250 g (9 oz) ramen noodles,
home-made (page 130) or
store bought

1 bunch of green
vegetables, washed and
cut into bite-sized pieces

shichimi togarashi, to serve

SERVES 2

FOR THE PLATED VERSION:

Wash the spring onions, then divide into the green and white parts. Shred the green bits and very thinly julienne the whites, keeping them separate.

After the duck has finished cooking on the skin side for 15 minutes, turn it over onto the flesh side and sear all the parts that appear uncooked. After you've seared each side, leave the duck on the meat side for a further minute (it should be 2 minutes in total), then transfer the duck and leek from the pan to a plate and allow to rest for 5 minutes. Take the pan off the heat, but do not wash.

After 5 minutes, place the pan back on the heat and turn the heat up to high. Add the spring onion greens and stir-fry until wilted. Add the soy sauce mixture and any accumulated juices under the duck. Allow to bubble until slightly thickened, then remove from the heat.

Slice the duck, then place on your serving dish with the leek. Pour the sauce over, garnish with the spring onion whites and serve.

FOR THE SOUP VERSION:

While the duck is cooking, bring the dashi to a simmer and prepare a pot of boiling water for cooking the noodles.

After the duck has finished cooking on the skin side for 15 minutes, very quickly sear the flesh side of the duck just to colour it, then remove from the pan with the leek. Don't worry if you think it's still raw; it will cook further in the soup.

Quickly blanch your vegetables in the boiling water; remove with tongs and place in a colander to drain. Boil the noodles in the same water, then pour into the colander to drain, shaking the colander to remove as much excess water as possible.

Divide the noodles and vegetables among bowls.

Add 3 tablespoons of the soy sauce mixture to the simmering dashi. Taste and add more of the dashi mixture, or salt, until you are happy with the flavour. Pour it over the noodles and top with the greens.

Slice the duck breast and fan it out over the noodles with the leek. Serve with shichimi togarashi for sprinkling over.

KAMO NEGI PHOTOGRAPHY OVERLEAF →

KAMO NEGI

鯛のﾏ
カジキ煮煮
鴨木ギ
ラーメン

本日のおすすめ

トマト和風らすやっ

胡瓜たたき

火明水ヨツパイ

TONTEKI

トンテキ SOY-BASTED GRILLED PORK STEAK

Simple and satisfying, these thick pork steaks with a umami-rich sauce are great for sharing, or for serving as individual meals, with a mound of shredded cabbage and rice, and some mayonnaise on the side.

2 pork scotch fillet steaks, 2.5 cm (1 inch) thick

salt and black pepper, for seasoning

3 tablespoons mirin

3 tablespoons soy sauce

3 tablespoons oyster sauce

3 tablespoons tomato sauce (ketchup)

1 tablespoon worcestershire sauce

½ tablespoon sugar

2 tablespoons neutral-flavoured oil

6 garlic cloves, finely sliced

SERVES 2

Using the end of a sharp knife, poke small holes into the pork steaks. Season with salt and pepper, then set aside to come to room temperature.

Mix together the mirin, soy sauce, oyster sauce, tomato sauce, worcestershire sauce and sugar. Set aside.

Add the oil to a large frying pan. Slowly fry the garlic slices over low heat for about 8–10 minutes, until browned. Using a slotted spoon, remove the garlic, leaving the oil in the pan, and place the garlic on paper towel to drain.

Heat the pan over high heat. Using paper towel, dry off any moisture on the pork steaks and carefully add them to the pan. (Cook the pork in batches if your pan cannot fit both steaks at once.)

Turn the heat down to medium–high and cook the steaks for 2–3 minutes per side, or until cooked to your liking. Remove the pork from the pan and set aside in a warm place to rest.

Meanwhile, drain the excess oil from the pan, then add the soy sauce mixture. Bring to the boil and cook for about 5 minutes, until thickened. Add the fried garlic slices, stir and remove from the heat.

Slice the pork, then arrange on plates and spoon the sauce over. Serve with a side salad or other small dishes.

YAKINIKU
焼肉

The big celebrations, catch-ups or blow-out meals for large groups often revolve around yakiniku, with co-workers and friends huddled around a hotplate full of sizzling meat and vegetables, alongside an array of side dishes and dipping sauces.

The star of the show is always wagyu – usually featuring two or three different cuts, such as sirloin, short rib and skirt steak, as well as intestines, and tongue, which may be the most prized part. Diners use the provided tongs to sear the meat on the scorching-hot central grill, then drop it into their individual sauces to eat with rice or on its own. The most common side dish is the Korean namul, the recipe for you'll find overleaf.

The end of the meal is signalled by the arrival of a nabe (stew), such as motsunabe (page 74). The nabes in these restaurants are some of the best in the city, using all the offcuts of the premium wagyu and simmering them for hours. Perfect to warm you before heading back out into the cool night air.

A GUIDE TO CREATING YOUR OWN YAKINIKU

Meat for yakiniku should be well marbled, and cut against the grain, about 1 cm (½ inch) thick – thin enough to cook quickly, yet thick enough that it can be cooked medium-rare, if the diner prefers. Plan for around 150 g (5½ oz) meat per person.

There are lots of different cuts for yakiniku, with some new ones emerging in recent years.

Some of the most popular are:

· sirloin (ロース)
· boneless short rib (カルビ)
· chuck short rib (三角バラ)
· skirt steak (ハラミ)
· chuck roll (ザブトン)
· bottom round (カイノミ)
· tongue (タン)

Chicken thigh and pork loin and belly also feature.

Seasonal vegetables are always included, sliced about 1 cm (½ inch) thick. Some recommendations are onion, carrot, pumpkin (winter squash), zucchini (courgette), capsicum (bell pepper), mushrooms and asparagus.

Below are some sauces to go with your yakiniku.

NEGI SHIO TARE ネギ塩タレ

4 spring onions (scallions), white and light green parts only, very finely chopped

60 ml (¼ cup) sesame oil

1 lemon, juiced

1 teaspoon salt

2 garlic cloves, grated

black pepper to taste

½ teaspoon chicken consommé powder (optional)

SERVES 4

Mix all the ingredients together and serve.

SPICY TARE 辛いタレ

¼ onion, grated

½ tablespoon grated fresh ginger

1 garlic clove, grated

1 tablespoon soy sauce

1 tablespoon sake

2 teaspoons sesame oil

1 teaspoon gochujang

½ teaspoon sugar

1 tablespoon grated sesame seeds

1 tablespoon whole roasted sesame seeds

SERVES 4

Mix all the ingredients together. Refrigerate and allow to mature for 3–5 days before using.

CONTINUED OVERLEAF →

RED WINE HONEY SOY TARE 赤ワインと蜂蜜ソース

200 ml (7 fl oz) red wine

100 ml (3½ fl oz) soy sauce

1 tablespoon honey

2 tablespoons sugar

¼ apple, grated

1 tablespoon grated
fresh ginger

1 tablespoon grated sesame

1 tablespoon sesame oil

1 teaspoon aka miso paste

Bring the red wine to the boil in a small saucepan, then cook until reduced by half. Add the soy sauce, honey and sugar. Simmer until the sugar has dissolved.

Remove from the heat and add the remaining ingredients, whisking to dissolve the miso paste.

Cool and refrigerate until required.

SERVES 4

NAMUL ナムル

1 tablespoon salt

400 g (14 oz) vegetables –
a mixture of bean sprouts,
carrots and spinach leaves

3 tablespoons sesame oil

2 tablespoons sesame
seeds

1 tablespoon soy sauce

2 garlic cloves, grated

1 spring onion (scallion),
white and light green part
only, thinly sliced

Bring a pot of water to the boil and add the salt.

Wash your vegetables. Peel and julienne the carrots.

Blanch the bean sprouts, carrot and spinach in the boiling water for 30 seconds. Drain and rinse in cold water. When cold, squeeze out the excess liquid from the vegetables.

Place the vegetables in a bowl with the remaining ingredients and mix together.

Cover and marinate for 15 minutes in the refrigerator before eating.

SERVES 4

OTHER CONDIMENT OPTIONS

Salt and pepper

Soy sauce

Wasabi (paste, or freshly
grated if available)

Lemon wedges

Ponzu and grated daikon

YAKINIKU PHOTOGRAPHY OVERLEAF →

YAKINIKU

MOTSUNABE

もつ鍋 OFFAL STEW

Steam rises from a large, urn-like pot in the centre of the izakaya, visible to everyone present; this must be the restaurant's signature dish. A mysterious concoction filled with what you suspect is meat, under a dark mahogany broth, not quite dark enough to be soy, so you assume it's miso, and a very dark miso at that – which can only mean strong flavours lurk beneath that bubbling surface.

Izakaya novices may wonder what's inside this stew that lands in front of happy customers, covered in chopped spring onion (another sign it's a potent brew), and be too afraid to try it. This would be a mistake, as many izakayas pride themselves on this dish, their motsunabe. Every restaurant's blend of meat and flavourings is unique to that restaurant and a secret recipe, possibly as old as the izakaya itself.

Motsunabe is classic izakaya fare, often employing the cheapest meats, such as beef or pork intestines, lungs and stomach, cooked slowly in a rich, miso-based broth with daikon and konnyaku, both of which are excellent at absorbing flavour while maintaining their structural integrity. Sometimes gochujang, Korean spicy bean paste, is added for kick, and each shop decides whether their blend includes more aka (red) miso to counter the strong flavours of the meat, or more shiro (white) miso, to add sweetness and let the flavour of the meat come through.

Few may know each restaurant's exact blend, but everyone knows that after a long day's work, there's little more fortifying than a piping-hot bowl from that mysterious, rippling cauldron.

1 kg (2 lb 3 oz) beef – a blend of intestines (from a reputable butcher) and brisket; you can use all brisket if you prefer, or all intestines if you're feeling adventurous

½ daikon, peeled, cut into bite-sized pieces

250 g (9 oz) konnyaku, torn into bite-sized pieces

a handful of rice

500 ml (2 cups) dashi (page 32)

75 g (2½ oz) zarame

75 g (2½ oz) aka miso paste

75 g (2½ oz) shiro miso paste

Place the beef in a large pot, cover with cold water and bring to the boil. Leave to boil for 10 minutes, then drain and rinse the beef to get rid of any foam.

While the beef is boiling, place the daikon and konnyaku in a separate pot. Cover with water, add the rice (this removes any bitterness from the daikon) and bring to the boil, then simmer for 5 minutes. Drain, discarding the rice.

Add the beef to a pressure cooker, along with the daikon and konnyaku. Add the remaining ingredients, except the potato starch and spring onion. Place the lid on securely and bring up to high pressure. Cook for 15 minutes, then remove from the heat and allow to return to normal pressure naturally. (If you don't have a pressure cooker, place the ingredients in a large pot, bring to the boil over high heat, then turn the temperature down to medium–low and simmer for 1½ hours.)

Remove the lid when safe to do so, then place the pressure cooker back on the stove, without the lid on. Bring to the boil, then leave to boil for 20 minutes.

25 g (1 oz) gochujang

15 ml (½ fl oz) soy sauce

2 knobs of fresh ginger,
peeled and grated

½ garlic bulb, peeled

2 tablespoons potato starch

1 bunch of spring onions
(scallions), finely sliced

SERVES 6

After 20 minutes, add 2 tablespoons water to the potato starch
to make a slurry, then pour it into the boiling broth. Stir and cook
for about 2–5 minutes, until thickened.

Remove from the heat, divide among bowls and serve topped
with the spring onion.

MIZU SHINGEN MOCHI
水信玄餅 RAINDROP CAKES

This may be called a 'cake' in English, but it is really a jelly. A jelly that is very lightly set using agar, and resembles a crystal-clear raindrop, accompanied by a flavoured syrup. I've gone with a matcha syrup for this recipe, but traditionally it is served with the black sugar syrup on page 188 and sprinkled with kinako (roasted soy bean flour).

A raindrop cake looks spectacular, and with the right moulds (spherical ice moulds or semicircular moulds) is very easy to prepare. This makes it a great, easy dessert for busy izakayas, and a refreshing end to a meal.

1 g (⅟₂₈ oz) kanten agar

400 ml (14 fl oz) water

80 g (2¾ oz) sugar

2 teaspoons matcha powder, plus extra for sprinkling

SERVES 4

Set out four small bowls or circular moulds, about 6 cm (2¼ inches) in diameter.

In a small saucepan, combine the agar, water and 20 g (¾ oz) of the sugar. Bring to a simmer, stirring constantly to dissolve the sugar and agar. Working quickly, so the liquid doesn't start solidifying in the pan, pour the mixture into the bowls, then refrigerate for at least 2 hours to set.

Make a matcha syrup by whisking together the matcha powder and remaining (60 g) sugar in a small bowl. Heat 30 ml (1 fl oz) water in a small saucepan until simmering, then slowly stream it into the matcha powder and sugar, whisking well.

Pour the mixture back into the saucepan and cook over low heat, just until the sugar has dissolved. Pour the syrup into a container and refrigerate.

When the cakes have set, unmould each one onto a serving plate. Spoon the matcha syrup around them, sprinkle a little matcha powder over and serve.

COCKTAILS
カクテル

Though the most commonly drunk beverage in an izakaya is still beer, there are many patrons who prefer a refreshing mixed drink with their meal. From a classic whisky highball to the invigorating lemon sour, there's a drink for any izakaya meal.

Here's a small selection for you to pair with the recipes from this book. The yuzucha is an especially good digestif.

WHISKY HIGHBALL

ice cubes

30 ml (1 fl oz) whisky

125 ml (½ cup) soda water (club soda)

1 slice of lemon (optional)

Fill a tall glass with ice.

Add the whisky, then the soda water and stir.

Finish with a lemon slice if desired.

SERVES 1

LEMON SOUR

ice cubes

½ teaspoon honey (optional), at warm room temperature

30 ml (1 fl oz) shochu

15 ml (½ fl oz) lemon juice

150 ml (5½ fl oz) tonic water

Fill a tall glass with ice.

If using the honey, mix it with the lemon juice until dissolved.

Pour the shochu over the ice, then the lemon juice, followed by the tonic water.

Stir well and serve.

SERVES 1

IZAKAYA 居酒屋

CASSIS ORANGE

30 ml (1 fl oz) crème de cassis

125 ml (½ cup) orange juice

1 slice of orange

SERVES 1

Pour the crème de cassis into a wine glass. Pour the orange juice over the back of a spoon to create a layer on top.

Finish with a slice of orange.

Serve with a stirrer for the drinker to combine the two liquids.

UME GINGER

½ teaspoon grated fresh ginger

80 ml (⅓ cup) ginger ale

40 ml (1½ fl oz) umeshu (ume/pickled plum liqueur)

SERVES 1

Squeeze the liquid from the grated ginger, reserving the liquid and discarding the pulp.

Combine all the ingredients in a short glass and stir.

YUZUCHA

30 ml (1 fl oz) yuzushu (yuzu liqueur)

125 ml (½ cup) hot black tea

SERVES 1

Pour the yuzushu and tea into a mug and stir. Serve hot.

MAKANAI

賄い料理

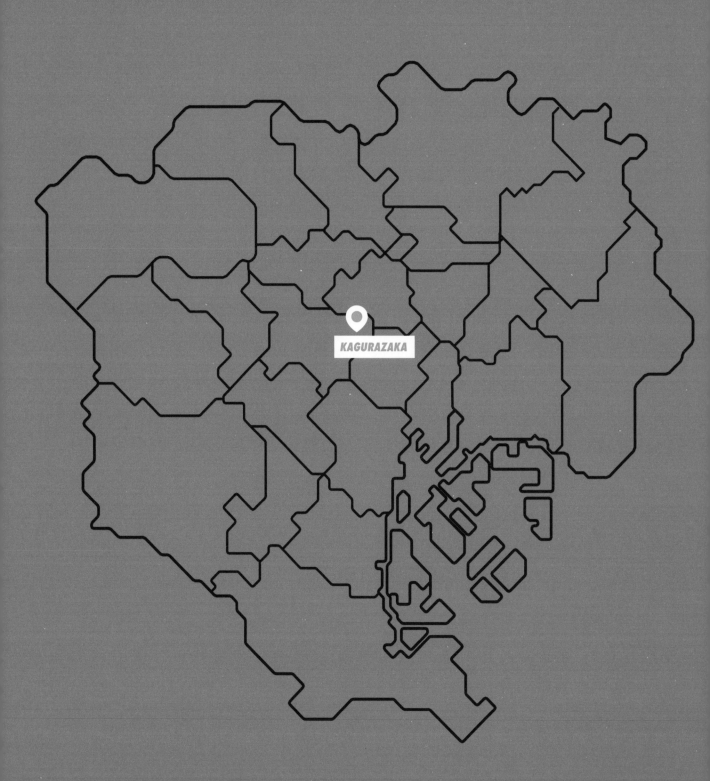
KAGURAZAKA

Once home to many geisha houses, Kagurazaka retains a lot of old-world charm missing from areas of Tokyo now dominated by skyscrapers. It has traditionally been a high-class district with many famous traditional and expensive restaurants.

お粗末様でした。

(Osomatsu sama deshita)*

The head chef bows deeply in the restaurant's entrance, farewelling the last customer of the night. The happy diners slowly trundle away in the dark. Looking back over their shoulders, they see the head chef still there, waving. They wave back before finally disappearing around the corner. ▶◀● Inside the restaurant, there's still a flurry of activity - waiters and waitresses washing and polishing glassware, vacuuming floors and tidying the seats and cushions. Cooks and kitchen hands scrubbing pots and pans, scouring stoves, walls and work benches, cleaning and drying the various antique plates and bowls used that evening.

●▶◀ You are in a small, already cleaned corner of the kitchen, away from the activity, looking down at the various ends and offcuts spread out on the counter. The soup chef has passed you some dashi, the sashimi chef handed over a saku (rectangle) of prized chutoro tuna, the grill chef a few pieces of wagyu, and you have a few handfuls of eggplant (aubergine) and mushrooms. Tonight, it is your job to make the end-of-night staff meal for the restaurant. It must be fast, use minimal equipment (you don't want to clean everything again!) and, above all, delicious. What will you do?

▶◀● This meal is called makanai, and it is one of the few perks of restaurant work in Japan. Long hours, six days a week and little pay are made more palatable if the restaurant you work at provides a generous makanai. ●▶◀ Makanai is usually taken twice a day. First, an hour or two before the first customer arrives for dinner, around 4 p.m., and then after everyone has packed up for the evening, 11 p.m. or later, depending on the restaurant's operating hours. In high-end restaurants, the meal can be taken very seriously as training for young chefs, with guidelines on what can be served. Traditional Japanese restaurants, for example, insist that only Japanese cuisine can be served for makanai. This is seen as a way of honing the employees' palate to be in tune with the food they're serving. It is also a training ground for new chefs to practise their craft and creativity, so they can one day advance up the ranks. Some restaurants take makanai so seriously that, at its conclusion, the chef who made it is summoned to the head chef's office and given a review of their performance and how they can improve.

▶◀● For the employees who aren't subjected to such pressure, though, makanai is a welcome break. It's a time when they can sit together, remove their hats and, in some restaurants where the staff room is covered in tatami mats, kick off their shoes and stretch their toes. Not all formality goes out the window, though: junior staff are required to pour drinks for the senior staff, and no one is allowed to leave until the head chef proclaims the end of the night. Despite this, workers still appreciate the chance to relax and talk about baseball or news. And then there's the food… ●▶◀ Cuts of premium sashimi-grade fish, wagyu beef, scallops, abalone, eel… anything that wasn't sold that day, or couldn't be sold – like a piece of beef that was not cut quite right – finds a second life as part of makanai. It's up to the skill of the chef whether or not those ingredients shine, becoming something worthy of being served at the restaurant, or wilt, destined for the trash can, leaving the staff with disappointment and hunger plastered on their faces. ▶◀● The best meals are quick and easy to make, with ingredients that can be subbed in and out without a decrease in deliciousness – dishes such as a fish collar hotpot (page 102), which can be made with a variety of fish collars, or ankake gohan (page 92), which can use almost any assortment of random ingredients and still taste fantastic. And while it's unlikely staff will find themselves sitting down to a wagyu steak or sashimi platter, it is quite possible (depending on what the restaurant serves), to find before them soy-simmered wagyu gyudon (page 107) or a kaleidoscopic chirashi zushi (page 96) that would be worth hundreds of dollars if the restaurant sold it. ●▶◀ *Maybe restaurant life isn't so bad after all?*

---

* *Osomatsu sama deshita* ('Sorry for the bad food') is the typically humble and modest Japanese way to respond to *Gochisosama deshita* ('Thanks for the food'). The English equivalent may be 'It wasn't much' or 'It was nothing'.

ANKAKE GOHAN

あんかけご飯 OMELETTE-WRAPPED RICE IN A THICK SAUCE

With just rice, stock and a few random ingredients, you can create one of the easiest and most delicious meals around. Ankake at its most basic is a stock, usually dashi or chicken stock, thickened with kuzu or potato starch, then poured over a carb. Ankake gohan is a firm makanai favourite because you can add any stir-fried meat, seafood or vegetables to the ankake sauce to create something filling, comforting, and greater than the sum of its parts.

For this recipe we are pouring the sauce over fried rice wrapped in an omelette, which is at the fancier end of the spectrum, but it's delicious over plain rice or fried noodles. The key is to have all the ingredients prepared and ready to go, as the final dish comes together very quickly. You don't want one part to get cold while you're making another.

oil, for frying

400 g (14 oz) meat, seafood and vegetables, cut into bite-sized chunks

ANKAKE SAUCE

500 ml (2 cups) dashi (page 32) or stock

2 tablespoons soy sauce

2 tablespoons sake

½ teaspoon oyster sauce

1 teaspoon rice vinegar

salt and white pepper, to taste

2 tablespoons potato starch

2 tablespoons water

FRIED RICE

oil, for frying

2 slices bacon, diced

½ cup vegetables, such as onion, carrot, peas, corn or capsicum (bell pepper), diced into 1 cm (½ inch) chunks

375 g (2 cups) cooked, cooled white rice

2 tablespoons chicken stock powder

OMELETTE

12 eggs, whisked

SERVES 4

First, make the ankake sauce by bringing the dashi or stock to the boil in a large saucepan, then adding the soy sauce, sake, oyster sauce and vinegar. Taste, then add salt, white pepper and more vinegar to taste. The sauce should be quite strong, as it will get slightly diluted by the other ingredients and rice.

Mix together the potato starch and water, then add to the boiling sauce. Mix well, bring back to the boil and cook over high heat for about 30 seconds to 1 minute, until visibly thickened. Turn off the heat and set the sauce aside.

Heat a large, non-stick frying pan over medium–high heat. Add some oil, then your chosen meat, seafood and vegetables. Cook until the protein is almost done, then add the mixture to the pot of ankake sauce. Stir to cover everything with the sauce, then set aside while we prepare the fried rice.

Wipe out the frying pan you just used and reheat on medium–high heat. Add some oil, then the bacon and vegetables. Stir-fry until cooked, then add the cooked rice. Use the back of a spoon or ladle to break the rice up into individual grains; you may need to add more oil. Stir the chicken stock powder through, then transfer to a large bowl.

Clean the frying pan, ready for the omelette. Bring the frying pan back to medium heat. Add 1 tablespoon oil, swirl the oil around the pan, then add one-quarter of the whisked eggs. Quickly cover the base of the pan evenly with the egg and cook for about 1–2 minutes, until the egg slides freely on the bottom of the pan.

Place one-quarter of the fried rice on the third of the omelette furthest away from you, then fold the omelette over to cover the rice. Transfer the omelette to a plate and keep warm. Repeat three more times with the remaining egg mixture and rice.

If necessary, reheat the sauce, then pour over the omelettes and serve.

GYU KOROKKE

牛コロッケ BEEF CROQUETTES

Over 95 per cent of makanai in Japanese restaurants involves something over rice. Japanese love rice, but sometimes it's nice to have a change.

This recipe takes the standard beef gyudon and makes it extra special by turning it into golden, crunchy croquettes. While bowls of gyudon may elicit an oishiso! ('looks delicious!') from the staff, seeing rows of perfectly shaped and fried croquettes never fails to garner anything less than a sugoi! ('wow!') from the gathering diners.

600 g (1 lb 5 oz) potatoes, peeled and roughly diced

salt and black pepper, for seasoning

1 quantity of gyudon (page 107), cold

¼ teaspoon ground nutmeg

150 g (1 cup) plain (all-purpose) flour

2 eggs, whisked

60 g (1 cup) panko breadcrumbs

1 litre (4 cups) neutral-flavoured oil, for deep-frying

shredded cabbage, to serve

tonkatsu sauce, to serve

MAKES 12 CROQUETTES

Place the potato in a saucepan and cover with cold water. Tip in a teaspoon of salt, then bring to the boil. Cook until soft (when the tip of a knife goes through easily), then tip into a colander to drain.

Meanwhile, strain off any liquid in the gyudon by placing it in a colander set over a bowl. Reserve the gyudon liquid and roughly chop the solids.

Gently mash the drained potato using a potato masher, leaving some chunks, and combine with the gyudon solids. Add in the reserved liquid, little by little. You want to add the flavour of the liquid without making the mixture too soft to shape into croquettes, so use your intuition to decide how much liquid to add. It should be a bread-dough consistency. Season the mixture with salt, pepper and nutmeg, tasting as you go.

Divide into 12 pieces and mould into the shapes shown, or any shape you desire. Place on a baking tray lined with baking paper, cover with plastic wrap and freeze for 3 hours, or overnight.

When ready to cook, prepare one tray with flour, one with the whisked eggs and one with the panko.

Crumb the frozen croquettes by firstly coating in the flour, then the eggs, then the panko. Place back on the lined baking tray while you heat up the oil.

Pour the oil into a large saucepan and heat to 170ºC (340ºF). Heat your oven to 160ºC (320ºF).

Fry the croquettes three at a time for 5 minutes, or until the croquettes are golden brown. Remove from the oil and allow to drain on a rack over a baking tray. Place the tray in the oven while you fry the remaining croquettes in batches.

When all the croquettes are fried, transfer them to the oven for at least 5 minutes to warm them through to the centre. Test the centre is hot by inserting a wooden skewer into the centre for 5 seconds, then checking that part of the skewer is hot.

Serve with the cabbage, passing the tonkatsu sauce separately.

CHIRASHI ZUSHI

ちらし寿司 SCATTERED SUSHI

Chirashi zushi, or 'scattered sushi', is without a doubt the king of makanai at sushi restaurants. It's something that, if sold, would bring in hundreds of dollars – but at the end of the night, when all the customers have left, becomes the employees' prize after a long day's work. Sushi restaurants always prepare everything for the guests fresh that morning, so anything that has been prepared that day but doesn't get sold usually contributes to the chirashi. It could comprise silky slices of tuna belly, colourful streaks of salmon and trout, pops of ikura or salmon roe, translucent ribbons of calamari or plump pieces of crab. All of this richness is perfectly balanced by crunchy cucumber, fresh avocado and the traditional sushi accompaniments of soy, wasabi and gari (pickled ginger).

The base layer of kinshi tamago (egg) and mushroom tsukudani sets the canvas for a good chirashi, to let the other ingredients shine.

300 g (10½ oz) sushi rice, uncooked

MUSHROOM TSUKUDANI

1 teaspoon soy sauce

1 teaspoon mirin

½ teaspoon sugar

200 ml (7 fl oz) dashi (page 32), dried shiitake mushroom rehydrating liquid, or water

200 g (7 oz) fresh shiitake mushrooms (or rehydrated dried shiitake; use the liquid instead of the dashi or water above)

3 cm (1¼ inch) square of kombu, preferably already used for making dashi

Prepare the mushroom tsukudani first, as it must be cooled before use. Bring the soy sauce, mirin, sugar and dashi to a simmer in a small saucepan. Dice the shiitake, then add to the pan along with the kombu and bring to the boil. Place a baking paper cartouche on top, reduce the heat and simmer for 10 minutes. Remove the cartouche, turn the heat up to medium–high and cook for 10 minutes more, checking and stirring regularly to ensure the pot doesn't boil dry. The liquid should have evaporated by two-thirds, and the mushrooms will be coated in a soy glaze. Remove from the heat and chill until cold. Drain before using.

Thoroughly mix together all the kinshi tamago ingredients, except the oil, well (using an electric mixer gives the best result); strain to remove any unblended egg.

Heat a non-stick frying pan or a 21 cm (8¼ inch) square tamago pan over medium heat and coat with a light layer of oil. Test the temperature by dropping in a little of the egg mixture: it should sizzle and cook in 2–3 seconds. Once the temperature is correct, pour in the egg mixture and swirl the pan to coat the base. Leave until the egg is fully set, then carefully flip it over by rolling one edge up over a chopstick, lifting and placing the other side down. Leave for 3–5 seconds, then remove to a chopping board. When cool, fold the bottom third up, then the top third over. Thinly slice and set aside.

KINSHI TAMAGO

2 eggs

1 teaspoon sugar

a pinch of salt

a pinch of potato starch

1 tablespoon neutral-flavoured oil

SUSHI VINEGAR

125 ml (½ cup) rice vinegar

30 g (1 oz) sugar

20 g (¾ oz) salt

3 cm (1¼ inch) square of kombu

TOPPINGS

200 g (7 oz) assorted seafood, such as tuna, salmon, kingfish, prawns (shrimp), crab, sea urchin and/or salmon roe, cut into 1 cm (½ inch) cubes

¼ cucumber, seeds removed, then cut into 1 cm (½ inch) cubes

½ avocado, flesh cut into 1 cm (½ inch) cubes

2 okra, blanched in boiling water for 2 minutes, then chilled and sliced

2 shiso leaves, shredded

TO SERVE

soy sauce

wasabi

pickled ginger

SERVES 4

Simmer all the sushi vinegar ingredients in a saucepan until the sugar and salt have dissolved. Remove from the heat and cool to room temperature. Measure out 100 ml (3½ fl oz) and reserve the rest for another day.

Cook the sushi rice according to the packet instructions, then place in a large bowl. If you have a friend nearby, have them fan the rice to cool it as you incorporate the sushi vinegar. Pour in one-third of the sushi vinegar and, using a rice paddle or flat wooden spoon, turn the rice. Pour in another one-third and fold again, trying to loosen any large clumps. Pour in the final one-third and fold, then, using a horizontal cutting motion – similar to dealing a playing card – cut the rice paddle through the rice to break up any clumps and evenly distribute the vinegar. Continue doing this until all the grains are separated and shiny from being coated in the sushi vinegar – but try to keep this process quite short. The longer it takes, the more the rice grains will break and the more stodgy the rice becomes. Spread the rice out over the bottom of the bowl. Place a clean, damp tea towel over the top and rest for 10 minutes.

Prepare your topping ingredients while the rice is resting.

When the rice is about body temperature, transfer to your serving dish. Top with the drained mushroom tsukudani, the egg and shiso. Scatter the remaining ingredients over the top in whatever fashion you choose.

Serve immediately, with soy sauce, wasabi and pickled ginger on the side.

CHIRASHI ZUSHI PHOTOGRAPHY OVERLEAF →

CHIRASHI ZUSHI

NASU NIBITASHI

茄子煮浸し DASHI-BRAISED EGGPLANT & SHIITAKE

A versatile vegetable braise that can be eaten hot or cold, this recipe uses eggplant and shiitake mushrooms, but can also feature okra, capsicum (bell pepper), greens and even tomato. The vegetables are pan-fried, to extract water, then immersed in a punchy broth of soy, vinegar, ginger and chilli. The liquid is absorbed by the ingredients as they cook and cool, making for a dish that is deeply flavoured, yet retains the texture of the vegetables.

500 g (1 lb 2 oz) eggplants (aubergines)

10 fresh shiitake mushrooms

2 tablespoons neutral-flavoured oil

200 ml (7 fl oz) dashi (page 32)

60 ml (¼ cup) soy sauce

60 ml (¼ cup) sake

1 tablespoon sugar

1 teaspoon rice vinegar

2 dried chillies, seeds removed, thinly sliced

1 tablespoon shredded fresh ginger

2 spring onions (scallions), sliced

SERVES 4 AS A SIDE DISH

Cut off and discard the top and bottom of the eggplants. Slice the eggplants in half lengthways, then score one-third deep in a crisscross fashion, with the score marks 1 cm (½ inch) apart. Cut into 10 cm x 3 cm (4 inch x 1¼ inch) wedges.

Clean the shiitake mushrooms, discard the stems and cut a cross in the caps.

In a large saucepan, heat the oil over medium heat. Add the eggplant and mushrooms in one layer and cook for about 3–5 minutes, turning, until all sides are coloured.

Mix together the remaining ingredients, except the spring onion, then add to the pan when the eggplant and mushroom are cooked and softened. Bring to the boil, then turn the heat down and simmer for 3 minutes.

Transfer to a dish and serve immediately, or chill in the refrigerator. Before serving, sprinkle with the spring onion.

KAMA NABE

カマ鍋 FISH COLLAR HOTPOT

One of the first lessons taught to Japanese chefs is the principle of mottainai – 'don't waste anything'. Apprentices learn very early on the importance of even a single grain of rice. Makanai is where this principle is most evident. Parts of the fish that cannot be turned into glistening jewel-like pieces of sushi become something more humble but just as delicious, savoured by the few behind the scenes.

Fish 'collars' are particularly prized. Their high fat content makes them tender and juicy when sprinkled with salt and grilled (shioyaki) or, as in this recipe, braised with an abundance of vegetables and tofu, to which rice is then added, to be softened and flavoured by the stewing liquid, resulting in a luscious savoury rice porridge (zosui). A fortifying meal before the train ride home.

500 g (1 lb 2 oz) fish collars (from your fishmonger)

500 g (1 lb 2 oz) tofu, cut into bite-sized pieces

500 g (1 lb 2 oz) Chinese cabbage (wombok), cut into large pieces

1 small daikon, peeled, cut in half lengthways, then sliced thinly

100 g (3½ oz) shiitake mushrooms, stems discarded

50 g (1¾ oz) shimeji mushrooms, ends discarded, torn into small pieces

½ bunch of spring onions (scallions), cut into 5 cm (2 inch) lengths

½ bunch of chrysanthemum greens

SOUP BASE

3 litres (12 cups) dashi (page 32)

125 ml (½ cup) soy sauce

165 ml (5½ fl oz) sake

¼ teaspoon salt, or to taste

ZOSUI

2 cups (370 g) cooked short-grain rice

2 eggs, whisked

2 spring onions (scallions), finely sliced

TO SERVE

ponzu (page 243)

shichimi togarashi

SERVES 4

Bring a pot of water to the boil. Add the fish collars for 10 seconds, then remove and plunge under cold running water. Using your fingers, carefully rub the fish (both the skin and meat) to get rid of any remaining scales and blood. Dry the fish collars and set aside.

Place all the soup base ingredients in a large saucepan (at least 4 litres/16 cups in size). Bring to the boil.

Add the fish collars, tofu, cabbage, daikon, mushrooms and spring onion and bring back to the boil. Turn the heat down to medium and cook at a gentle bubble for 5 minutes. Stir in the chrysanthemum greens, turn the heat to low and cook for a further 2 minutes.

Using a strainer or large slotted spoon, remove all the ingredients from the pot, reserving about 1.5 litres (6 cups) of the broth for the zosui, and arrange on a platter. Enjoy the fish and vegetables with ponzu for dipping, and shichimi togarashi for sprinkling over.

When you're ready for the zosui, bring the reserved broth to the boil. Add the rice, gently stirring to separate the grains, then return to the boil. Slowly pour in the egg, then turn off the heat. Once the egg has set, ladle into bowls and serve sprinkled with the spring onion.

SAKANA KARAAGE

魚唐揚げ FISH KARAAGE

At one Japanese restaurant I worked in, every staff meal was fish karaage, accompanied by shredded cabbage, steamed white rice and Kewpie mayonnaise. Every. Single. Day. And it speaks volumes that we never got sick of it.

The marinated fish with a shatteringly brittle crust, the silky, slightly acidic mayo, and refreshing bite of cabbage combine to create something addictive. Hot, fresh, pillowy rice provides the final, comforting touch.

2 tablespoons sake

2 tablespoons soy sauce

1 cm (½ inch) piece of fresh ginger, peeled and grated

200 g (7 oz) fresh white fish slices, 1–2 cm (½–¾ inch) thick, skinless and boneless

1 litre (4 cups) oil, for deep-frying

100 g (½ cup) potato starch, for coating

salt, for sprinkling

¼ head savoy cabbage

mayonnaise (home-made or your preferred brand), to serve

hot cooked rice, to serve

1 lemon, cut into wedges

SERVES 2

Combine the sake, soy sauce and ginger in a bowl, then massage into the fish slices. Cover and leave to marinate for 10 minutes.

Pour the oil into a pot with sides at least double the height of the oil. Heat to 180°C (350°F), or until the end of a wooden chopstick inserted into the oil bubbles vigorously.

Remove the fish from the marinade, dry thoroughly with paper towel, then coat in the potato starch, ensuring it is completely covered.

Carefully place the fish slices individually into the oil. Do not touch for the first 30 seconds, to allow the potato starch coating to set, then stir quickly to separate the slices if they are clumping together. Cook for 1–2 minutes more, depending on their thickness, then remove and drain on paper towel. Sprinkle with a little salt.

Serve warm, with the cabbage, mayonnaise, rice and lemon.

GYUDON
牛丼 STEWED BEEF OVER RICE

This recipe encapsulates good makanai cooking. The hands-on time could be 5 minutes or less, depending on how fast you can slice an onion (and if the beef is already sliced), and the results can be spectacular. There are versions of gyudon that include more ingredients, but this one relies on the quality of the beef to make it one of the purest and best. There is no water added to this recipe; the broth is simply the juices released by the beef and onion blending together with the soy, mirin and sake to create a wonderfully rich sauce.

Japanese restaurants will buy large pieces of beef, which are then cut down into steaks or slices for the customer. Any pieces of beef that are an odd shape or not the right weight are often thinly sliced and turned into this very dish. Wagyu will give the best end result, because the fat will keep it very tender through the simmering process, but any beef with good marbling, sliced thinly, will work.

1 tablespoon neutral-flavoured oil or rendered beef fat (see notes)

½ onion, sliced into 1 cm (½ inch) thick slices

300 g (10½ oz) beef, sliced about 3 mm (⅛ inch) thick against the grain (see notes)

100 ml (3½ fl oz) sake

30 ml (1 fl oz) mirin

70 ml (2¼ fl oz) soy sauce

1 tablespoon zarame or sugar

hot cooked rice, to serve

TOPPING OPTIONS

onsen eggs (page 242)

beni shoga (sliced pickled ginger)

sliced spring onions (scallions)

shichimi togarashi

ground sansho pepper

Heat a medium saucepan over medium heat, then add the oil or rendered beef fat. Add the onion and stir-fry for about 5 minutes, until softened but not coloured, then set aside in a small bowl, keeping the oil in the pan.

Add the beef to the saucepan and stir-fry for about 2–3 minutes, until coloured. Return the onion to the pan, along with the sake, mirin, soy sauce and zarame. Bring to the boil, skim off any scum that floats to the surface, then simmer for 5–10 minutes, or until the beef is soft and the sauce has cooked down slightly.

Remove from the heat, ladle over hot rice and serve with toppings of your choice.

NOTES: *Using a higher-quality secondary cut of beef is better in this recipe than using a low-quality sirloin or ribeye. Beef chuck is a good, inexpensive option.*

Restaurants often have a lot of rendered beef fat from trimmings. You can make your own by placing some beef trimmings in a deep saucepan and covering with water, then simmering until the water has evaporated and the trimmings have released all their oil, stirring occasionally so they don't catch on the bottom and burn. Strain, discarding the solids and reserving the liquid. This is your rendered beef fat.

SERVES 2

HIYAJIRU

冷や汁 RICE & TOPPINGS WITH CHILLED SESAME SOUP

This dish is really surprising. Pouring an ice-cold soup over warm rice is a concept that sounds like it shouldn't work. When I tried this on a summer's night, the cold dashi mixed with the warm rice created the perfect balance of hot and cold. The contrasting temperatures were also complemented by contrasting textures of soft rice and tender mackerel with crunchy cucumber, sesame seeds and nori. Sitting down to this dish after coming out of a hot restaurant kitchen felt like a sudden cooling breeze on a warm evening.

Try it when the mercury rises. I hope you feel the same sense of refreshment and revitalisation.

1 saba or salmon fillet,
1 salad chicken breast
(page 242) or a 600 g
(1 lb 5 oz) block of
momen tofu

salt, for seasoning

1 nori sheet

10 cm (4 inch) piece of
daikon

hot cooked rice, to serve

1 piece of myoga, or a
2 cm (¾ inch) piece of fresh
ginger, julienned

4 spring onions (scallions),
finely sliced

8 shiso leaves, shredded

1 tablespoon sesame seeds

PICKLED CUCUMBER

1 Lebanese (short)
cucumber, thinly sliced

1 tablespoon salt

SESAME DASHI

2 tablespoons sesame or
tahini paste

2 teaspoons shiro
miso paste

2 teaspoons aka miso paste

2 tablespoons mirin

300 ml (10 fl oz) dashi
(page 32), chilled

2 tablespoons toasted
sesame seeds

SERVES 2

First, cook your chosen protein. If using fish, generously salt both sides and pan-fry until cooked all the way through. Remove from the pan, then cool to room temperature. Using your hands or two forks, flake into large pieces and set aside.

For a salad chicken breast, dice it into 1 cm (½ inch) chunks.

If using tofu, simply drain it and break into bite-sized chunks. Place your chosen protein in the refrigerator for later use.

To pickle the cucumber, place it in a colander and sprinkle with the salt, then massage in lightly. Leave in the colander while you assemble the rest of the dish.

For the sesame dashi, mix the sesame paste and miso pastes in a bowl. Add the mirin and mix until homogenous. Pour in the dashi and mix until smooth and uniform, then add the sesame seeds. Pour into a serving vessel and set aside in the refrigerator.

Toast the nori sheet by waving it quickly over a stovetop flame, being very careful not to set it alight. It should turn crisp. Break into small pieces and place in a serving bowl.

Peel and grate the daikon. Place the grated daikon on a sheet of paper towel or a clean tea towel, bring the sides up and gently squeeze the daikon to remove some of the liquid. Squeeze the salted cucumber slices in the same manner.

Place the hot rice in bowls. On top, however you like, arrange your chosen protein, pickled cucumber, daikon and remaining toppings, leaving off the nori.

Serve with the sesame dashi on the side to pour over the rice, and the nori to sprinkle over at the end to retain the crunch.

MISO SOUP

味噌汁

The classic miso soup is served with almost every meal in Japanese restaurants. Simple to prepare, filling and healthy, this soup, when made well, is all at once savoury, sweet and full of umami – the ideal complement to prime the palate before the vinegary tang of the sushi rice in chirashi zushi (page 96).

800 ml (27 fl oz) dashi (page 32)

35 g (1¼ oz) shiro miso paste

30 g (1 oz) aka miso paste

1 tablespoon soy sauce

salt, to taste

4 tablespoons cubed silken tofu

4 tablespoons thinly sliced spring onion (scallion)

SERVES 4

Pour the dashi into a saucepan.

Place the miso pastes into a fine strainer, then immerse the strainer into the dashi broth. Using a whisk, blend the miso paste into the broth. Discard any solids left in the strainer.

Bring to a gentle simmer and add the soy sauce. Taste and add salt if required.

Distribute the tofu and spring onion between soup bowls, then ladle in the miso broth and serve.

OKOWA

おこわ STEAMED CHESTNUT STICKY RICE

Even in a concrete jungle like Tokyo, the aroma and taste of this steamed glutinous rice, full of seasonal ingredients and scented with bamboo leaves, is enough to take your mind to a forest with the dewy smell of recently fallen rain, wet leaves crunching underfoot, bamboo towers swaying gently in the breeze.

Extremely comforting, filling and healthy, okowa makes an easy weeknight meal that feels like a luxury. Any leftovers are even better the next day, as the flavours further meld together, increasing the harmony of the dish.

400 g (14 oz) glutinous rice

4 bamboo leaves (optional)

80 g (2¾ oz) cooked, peeled chestnuts

4 fresh shiitake mushrooms, or 4 rehydrated dried shiitake, cut into 5 mm (¼ inch) dice

1 carrot, cut into 5 mm (¼ inch) dice

2 pieces of aburaage tofu (fried tofu pouches), cut into 5 mm (¼ inch) dice

a handful of ginkgo nuts

2 tablespoons soy sauce

2 tablespoons mirin

2 tablespoons sake

1 tablespoon sesame oil

2 teaspoons salt

80 g (2¾ oz) chashu (page 128), cut into 5 mm (¼ inch) dice (optional)

SERVES 4

Wash the glutinous rice, transfer to a container, cover with 2 cm (¾ inch) cold water and refrigerate overnight.

The next day, line a steamer basket with a clean tea towel. Lay two bamboo leaves on top, if using. (If you are not using the leaves, use a round of baking paper with a few holes punched in it to let the steam pass through; this prevents the rice sticking to the tea towel.) Drain the glutinous rice and spread it around the steamer basket. Using your finger, create holes in the rice for the steam to pass through. Lay the remaining two bamboo leaves on top, if using, then fold the tea towel over.

Place the steamer over a saucepan of boiling water, put the lid on and steam for 20 minutes.

Meanwhile, mix the remaining ingredients together in a large bowl.

After 20 minutes, remove the tea towel and rice from the steamer. Mix the rice with the other ingredients.

Place the tea towel back in the steamer basket and cover with two bamboo leaves, if using. Cover with the rice mixture, again poking holes through for the steam. Cover with the remaining two bamboo leaves, if using, then fold the tea towel over the top and put the lid back on.

Place back over the boiling water for a further 20 minutes. Test the rice: if it is still hard in the centre, check there's still water in the pan and steam for another 10 minutes.

Serve the dish in the centre of the table, the smell of bamboo leaves permeating the dining room.

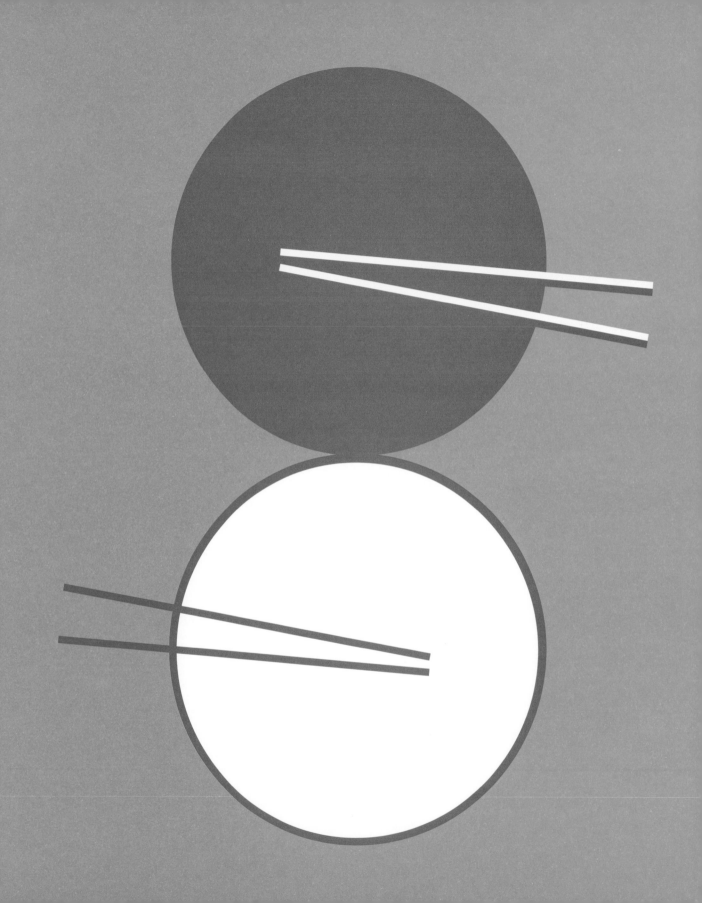

FAST FOOD
ファストフード

ROPPONGI

A nightlife area of Tokyo, clubs, bars and restaurants operate late into the night in Roppongi. In areas such as this, there is always a plentiful supply of cheap, fast food to fuel party-goers before their night starts, or to feed those looking for something to absorb the alcohol before travelling home.

麺の硬さ:

- ☐ やわ
- ☐ 普通
- ☑ かた
- ☐ 針金

NOODLE HARDNESS:
MEN NO KATASA:

SOFT	NORMAL	HARD	HARDWIRE
☐ Yawa	☐ Futsuu	☑ Kata	☐ Harigane

You look down at your watch; the minutes are ticking away before the last train leaves the station. In your mind you map out the route, and within moments you identify your target: a small ramen-ya a stone's throw from the station. Making haste, you rush there, jam a screwed-up ¥1000 bill into the ordering vending machine and punch in your order:

味玉つけめん ¥750 (Ajitama tsukemen)

チャーシュー ¥250 (Chashu)

Within minutes, you have before you a steaming-hot katsuobushi (bonito) and pork-dense broth, inside which floats a glossy soy-marinated egg and thick batons of chashu (pork), along with a plate of thick, slippery, chewy noodles, cooked to a toothsome bite. You pick up a few strands of noodles, swish them around in the hot broth and slurp them down noisily. It's rich, porky and savoury. The mound of ground katsuobushi in the broth adds a hint of smokiness, umami and just enough fish flavour to balance out the pork. Just how you like it. *Gochisosama deshita!* ('Thank you for the meal!' / 'It was a feast!')

▶◀● Izakayas are taking in their norens (door curtains) and closing their doors. Across the city, store-sign lights are going out, but some small ones are staying on or flickering into life at this late hour of the evening. International chain restaurants feature at this time, of course, but a smattering of small establishments, most not more than a few metres square, spring up in the narrow back alleys, near train stations, or even on train station platforms. If you've ever been to Japan, you'll be familiar with the tiny udon and soba stalls in the centre of train platforms and wondered how they can make anything in a space so small. ●▶◀ This is the time of the multinational and the micro restaurant. The latter is usually staffed by one person, often the owner, whose life, dreams and ambitions are all contained within the 15 square metres of their shop (Japanese salarymen

often transition into ramen store ownership to escape the rat race). It's highly likely they have spent the whole day meticulously caring for their ramen broth, or vigorously stirring their tonkatsu (cloudy pork) soup or carefully skimming their chintan (clear) soup, with any other time dedicated to making the juiciest chashu, and the most complex tare and flavourful oil. ◗◖● Across the road at the udon store, the chef is caressing his noodle dough, gently massaging it as if to tease out some extra deliciousness from this simple combination of flour and water. The udon store owner isn't concerned with tares and oils; all that matters to them is the noodle and the dashi. A noodle that should be smooth, chewy and firm, and always uniformly shaped (it would be a crime to serve uneven noodles), served with a dashi as clean-tasting as an ocean breeze, from the slow steeping of kombu and precise selection of the best katsuobushi, shaved that afternoon for peak freshness. At its simplest, it's served with a raw egg yolk dropped in the centre for tamago kake udon, or with a sheet of braised tofu draped over the top like a blanket, for kitsune udon. Tempura udon is udon at its most impressive, though – freshly fried jumbo prawns (shrimp), tails reaching skyward over a melody of seasonal vegetables, somehow perfectly cooked in their crisp, golden crust. The batter slowly slightly softens in the soup, losing a little crispness, but gaining all the flavour of the dashi. This is one of the unique joys of tempura udon. ●◗◖ It's not all noodles, though. Curry also plays a big part in late-night food culture. The demographic for curry usually skews younger, and if you go to a late-night curry house in Tokyo you'll understand why. The curry is used only as a sauce for lubricating the copious amount of fried food and rice these places serve. Pork katsu on top of croquettes on top of fried chicken – these are places for vast quantities of carbs and protein without sacrificing flavour. Japanese curry is sweet and mild compared to other curries around the world, but still complex and rich from the blend of spices and addition of honey and butter. ◗◖● Speaking of fried food, panko-crumbed delights in the form of kushikatsu have a home at this time also. Skewered, breaded and fried meat, fish and vegetables – as well as camembert cheese – are on offer. The best examples of kushikatsu are not greasy at all, a thin skin of shatteringly fragile breadcrumbs giving way to a delicately steamed mouthful within – all served with a slightly sweet, savoury communal sauce that serves to flavour and slightly cool the exterior of the freshly fried bite. ▶◀● All of the above are designed to be ordered, served and eaten in as little time possible. To give the customers a quick, satisfying meal before catching the last train home.

TONKOTSU RAMEN

豚骨ラーメン

A style of ramen that supposedly originated in Kyushu (Japan's South Island) when a ramen store owner accidentally boiled pork bones for hours instead of gently simmering them. The resulting soup was cloudy and thick, not at all like the thin, clear soup he had set out to make. Instead of throwing the soup out, he tried to save it by straining and seasoning it as he would a normal ramen soup. The result was more flavourful and delicious than his original version, with a luxurious viscosity from everything melting down and emulsyfying into the soup. Thus, he began making this new style of ramen, tonkotsu (pork bone) ramen, which has exploded in popularity and spread around the world.

This and the following recipes give instruction on creating a traditional tonkotsu ramen. It may look like a lot of work, but the results are worth it and any leftovers freeze well.

Instead of making a separate tare and oil (as a ramen shop would), to simplify things we're using the chashu cooking liquid from page 129, and the oil that separates from it, as the flavourings.

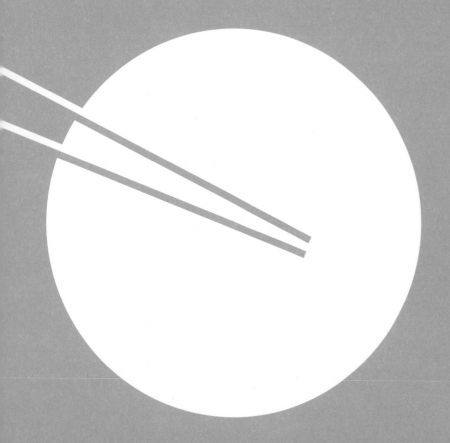

1 quantity of tonkotsu ramen broth (page 126)

dashi (page 32), as needed

1 quantity of ramen noodles (page 130)

salt, for seasoning

125 ml (½ cup) reserved chashu cooking liquid (page 129)

4 slices of chashu, warmed (page 129)

4 ramen eggs (page 129)

TOPPINGS (OPTIONAL)

ground sesame seeds

takana (pickled mustard greens)

beni shoga (shredded pickled ginger)

kikurage (black fungus mushroom), stir-fried with sake, soy sauce, chilli oil and sesame oil

spring onion (scallion), finely sliced

nori sheets

blanched cabbage and bean sprouts

flavoured oils such as chilli oil or spring onion oil (page 243), or oil that floats to the surface from the chashu

ground katsuobushi or other dried fish

SERVES 4

Measure the tonkotsu broth and add enough dashi to make 1.4 litres (47 fl oz). Pour it into a saucepan and heat it up. If the broth is too thick, add some more dashi to thin it out.

Meanwhile, boil the noodles for 4 minutes, then drain thoroughly.

Ladle the chashu liquid into four bowls. Add ½ teaspoon salt to each bowl.

Now pour 300 ml (10 fl oz) of the hot tonkotsu broth into your own bowl. Taste, then add more salt, dashi and chashu liquid as needed before you fill the other bowls. When you're happy, fill the rest of the bowls accordingly, then divide the noodles among the bowls.

Top with the chashu, ramen eggs and toppings of your choice.

TONKOTSU RAMEN BROTH
とんこつラーメンスープ

This is not a lazy weeknight dinner recipe. Tonkotsu ('pork bone') ramen is the most labour-intensive ramen around, but has become the most sought-after ramen style in Japan.

Tonkotsu can be very heavy and porky, a taste that can remind you of a ramshackle food stall in the back alleys of Kyushu, the birthplace of tonkotsu – but it can also be light and refined, as served in the fashionable high streets of Ginza with seasonal organic vegetables and kurobuta pork. The result largely depends on how far you want to cook the broth down, and which part of the pork you have chosen to use.

This recipe should give a medium-bodied tonkotsu, but feel free to adjust the consistency and flavour to your liking at the end.

This is something ramen shop owners have to do every day in preparation for opening – many of them starting with 120 litre (30 gallon) stockpots and stirring until the pork bones almost disintegrate. So, the next time you're lucky enough to sit down to a bowl of tonkotsu, after you've eaten and you see the owner methodically still stirring his pot, give him a small, appreciative bow and a loud Gochisosama deshita! ('Thank you for the meal!') in appreciation of his efforts.

EQUIPMENT

10 litre (40 cup) heavy-based stockpot (a heavy base will reduce the risk of the stock burning on the bottom)

long wooden spoon or paddle that can reach the bottom of the stockpot

large colander/strainer

INGREDIENTS

2.5 kg (5½ lb) pork marrow bones (back bones or knuckles); ask your butcher to cut these into 10 cm (4 inch) lengths, or as small as they can safely manage

1 pork trotter, split in half lengthways

MAKES 2.5 LITRES (10 CUPS)

Place the bones and trotter in the stockpot and cover with cold water. Bring to the boil, then drain and rinse the bones, cleaning them throughly with a scouring pad to remove any scum or blood.

Place the cleaned bones back into the stockpot. Add twice the weight of your ingredients in cold water, then bring to the boil.

Remove the grey scum that floats to the surface.

After about 30 minutes of boiling there should be no more grey scum. Anything that comes to the surface now should be white; this is fine and does not need to be removed. Give the pot a stir with your long spoon or paddle. Stir all the way from the bottom to the top, scraping clean the bottom of the pot so that nothing sticks and burns.

Boil for another 15 minutes, skimming off any grey scum that floats to the surface.

Using the long spoon or paddle, carefully stir the pot, again stirring from the bottom so that nothing burns.

In a traditional ramen store, someone would stand by the pot, constantly stirring for the next 8 hours. To make things easier for yourself, keep the pot on a medium–high heat and come back and stir every 5–10 minutes to ensure nothing is sticking to the bottom, and to start to extract some of the marrow from the bones.

After an hour of boiling, you should be able to break the remaining meat off the bones using your spoon or paddle. Do this carefully. This will speed up the cooking process.

Keep stirring and checking until the broth is very white. When you pull up some of the bones from the pot, they should be completely clean and free of any meat and bone marrow. During boiling, you may need to add more water to keep the bones submerged (see note). This process should take about 4 hours, depending on how vigorously you stir and the temperature of your stove. (More stirring and a higher temperature makes the process faster, but also increases the chances of burning.)

Turn off the heat. Using a large slotted spoon, remove the bones from the pot and discard them. Carefully strain the liquid through a large strainer, pressing down with the back of a ladle to extract as much liquid as possible. Use immediately, or cool and store in the refrigerator for up to 5 days.

NOTE: *The goal of making tonkotsu isn't gentle flavour extraction and reduction, as it is in a Western soup. Instead, it's using heat to break all the meat, fat and collagen down into the liquid – so refilling the pot with a little water to keep everything submerged and boiling is fine. Modern ramen stores use very large pressure cookers for this purpose. Domestic pressure cookers are usually too small, so the yield is generally not worth the effort. Also, it's fun to make it the old-fashioned way!*

CHASHU TO AJITAMA
チャーシューと味玉
CHASHU & RAMEN EGGS

A well-made piece of chashu has a great many uses. It can be chopped and added to fried rice or stir-fried vegetables, grilled in large steaks, or sliced thinly and used atop ramen noodles, as we have done here. Everyone's preference for chashu is different. Should it be lightly seasoned, or should the flavourings penetrate deep into the pork? Rolled or straight? Please use this as a base recipe and adjust to your taste by increasing or decreasing liquids, and adding or subtracting ingredients as you like.

CHASHU

1 kg (2 lb 3 oz) pork belly, skin and bones removed

2 tablespoons neutral-flavoured oil

200 ml (7 fl oz) soy sauce

45 ml (1½ fl oz) sake

30 ml (1 fl oz) mirin

60 g (2 oz) sugar

½ onion, cut into large chunks

4 garlic cloves, peeled

2 cm (¾ inch) piece of fresh ginger, sliced

1 dried chilli

a handful of spring onion (scallion) tops

RAMEN EGGS

6 eggs

SERVES 4, WITH LEFTOVERS

For the chashu, place the pork belly in a large saucepan and cover with water. Bring to the boil, then boil for 5 minutes. Drain the pork, discarding the water. Clean the saucepan.

Rinse the pork belly and place back in the clean saucepan, fat side down. Cover with 1.5 litres (6 cups) water.

Bring to the boil, cover with a baking paper cartouche, then simmer over medium–low heat for 90 minutes, or until a knife goes through the pork easily.

Drain the pork, reserving 1 litre (4 cups) of the liquid. Thoroughly dry the pork.

In a frying pan, heat the oil to medium–high, then sear the pork on all sides, being careful not to break the belly.

When browned on all sides, transfer the pork to a saucepan. Add the reserved liquid and the remaining chashu ingredients. Bring to the boil, cover again with a cartouche, then simmer for 60 minutes. Remove from the heat.

Transfer the pork and liquid to a lidded container, discarding the onion, garlic, ginger, chilli and spring onion.

To make the ramen eggs, bring a pot of water to the boil and boil the eggs for 6 minutes. Place the eggs in iced water, or run under cold water until room temperature. Carefully peel off the shells.

Place the eggs into the container with the pork, covering them as best you can with the liquid. Place a clean paper towel on top to help submerge the eggs. Refrigerate overnight.

The next day, remove the pork from the liquid and slice 1 cm (½ inch) thick for serving (see note). The ramen eggs are also ready to use. Keep the liquid as your flavouring for your ramen broth.

NOTE: *If you have a kitchen blow torch, you can char the pork slices for a better flavour. This can also be achieved on a barbecue or in a frying pan, but be careful not to cook the pork too long as the pieces are prone to falling apart. Alternatively, you can gently poach the pork in hot water, or roast in a 160°C (320°F) oven for 5–8 minutes.*

RAMEN NOODLES

麺

It is entirely possible to use store-bought ramen noodles instead of making your own, but unless you have access to high-quality fresh ramen noodles, you're better off making them yourself. This recipe results in wonderfully chewy noodles, with extra flavour and texture from the addition of wholemeal flour.

12 g (⅓ oz) food-grade lye powder, such as potassium carbonate and/or sodium carbonate

300 ml (10 fl oz) water

600 g (1 lb 5 oz) flour, either white plain (all-purpose) flour, or a mix of flours, such as 90% white and 10% wholemeal (whole-wheat)

1 teaspoon salt

potato starch, for dusting

SERVES 4

Whisk together the lye powder and water to make lye water.

Place the flour and salt in a deep bowl and slowly trickle in the lye water. Mix by hand until it becomes dough-like; add a little more water if it feels too tough to knead.

Roll the dough out into a large rectangle. With a wide side facing you, fold the left third over onto the centre, then the right side over to completely cover. Roll out again into a large rectangle, cover with plastic wrap and refrigerate for at least 20 minutes to let the dough rest.

Place the rested dough back on a clean bench and roll it out into a larger rectangle; you will find the dough can be rolled thinner this time. Cover and rest again for at least another 20 minutes.

Repeat the process of rolling and chilling until the dough is about 3 mm (⅛ inch) thick.

With a wide side of the rectangle facing you, dust the dough very liberally with potato starch. Fold the bottom half up over the top, dust with starch again, then fold in half once more. You should have a thin and long piece of dough in front of you.

Using a knife dusted with potato starch, cut the dough into noodles about 3 mm (⅛ inch) wide.

Dust the noodles again with starch and shake to separate into individual strands. (If making the noodles ahead, lay them on a tray, cover tightly with plastic wrap and refrigerate for up to 3 days.)

To serve, cook in plenty of boiling water for 4 minutes, or until done to your liking.

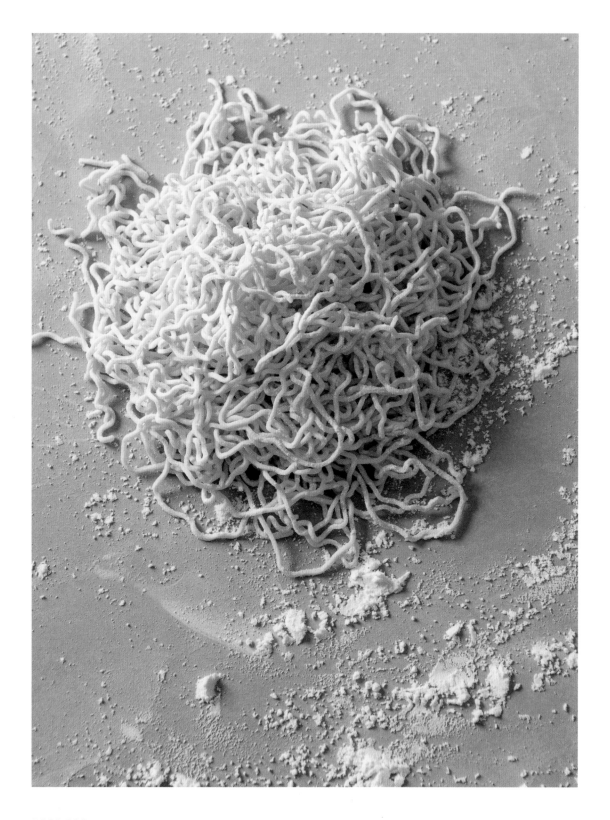

TANTANMEN
坦々麺

Tantanmen and ramen, although two sides of the same coin, are almost never served in the same restaurant. Whereas ramen is considered a Japanese take on Chinese noodles and is served in Japanese restaurants, tantanmen is still considered deeply Chinese and is only served in Chinese restaurants and tantanmen specialist spots.

Japanese tantanmen differs significantly from its origins, dandanmien, in China. In China, the noodles are quite dry, with a meat sauce similar to a spaghetti bolognese; Japan's version is, instead, a soup noodle. Both versions, however, feature a savoury minced meat, heavily seasoned with numbing pepper and bean paste, slicked with chilli oil, clinging to steamy, fresh noodles – with a little bit of fresh greens to balance the meal.

1 bunch of Chinese mustard greens (komatsuna), or other Asian green leafy vegetable, washed

500 g (1 lb 2 oz) ramen noodles, home-made (page 130) or store-bought

NIKUMISO

2 tablespoons neutral-flavoured oil

250 g (9 oz) minced (ground) pork or chicken

2 tablespoons tenmenjan or hoisin sauce

1 tablespoon tobanjan

1 teaspoon aka miso paste

1 cm (½ inch) piece of fresh ginger, peeled and finely grated

1 garlic clove, finely chopped

2 tablespoons sake

SOUP

4 tablespoons sesame paste

2 tablespoons soy sauce

2 tablespoons chinkiang black vinegar (or use 1 tablespoon rice vinegar if unavailable)

2 tablespoons roasted sesame oil

500 ml (2 cups) dashi (page 32)

500 ml (2 cups) soy milk

TOPPINGS

chilli oil

ground sansho pepper

roasted sesame oil

crushed sesame seeds

SERVES 4

For the nikumiso, heat a frying pan over medium–high heat. Add the oil, then the pork or chicken. Stir-fry until the meat is browned, using the back of a spoon to break up any large chunks; the meat should be uniformly broken into small bits.

Add the tenmenjan, tobanjan, miso paste, ginger and garlic and cook until the meat is fully coated and the sauce slightly thickened.

Stir in the sake and scrape up any bits that may be stuck to the pan. Reduce the sake slightly, then remove the nikumiso from the heat (see note). Set aside.

For the soup, mix together the sesame paste, soy sauce, vinegar and sesame oil. Divide among four soup bowls.

Bring a pot of water to the boil for cooking the noodles and vegetables.

Add the mustard greens to the boiling water for 30 seconds, then remove and drain. Cut into roughly 5 cm (2 inch) lengths.

Add the noodles to the boiling water and cook for 4 minutes, or according to the packet instructions. Drain well.

Meanwhile, finish preparing the soup. Bring the dashi and soy milk to a simmer in a large saucepan; do not boil as the soy milk will curdle. Ladle into the soup bowls and whisk into the sesame paste mixture.

Add the noodles, followed by 1 tablespoon nikumiso and the greens. Finish with toppings of your choice.

NOTE: *The nikumiso can be prepared up to 3 days in advance and refrigerated. It can also be used as a topping for rice.*

YUZU KOSHO CHICKEN RAMEN

柚子胡椒鳥ラーメン

In the Tokyo district of Ebisu, a store called Afuri pioneered this type of lighter, yuzu-scented ramen, which made ramen more accessible for those who had previously considered ramen to be too strongly flavoured, salty and rich. It's also a great option late at night for those wanting a more delicate soup.

This recipe is a fresh, spicy and simplified take on their chicken ramen. It's light and invigorating with the use of yuzu kosho (yuzu chilli paste), yuzu juice, a clear soup and fresh vegetables.

600 g (1 lb 5 oz) ramen noodles, home-made (page 130) or store-bought

2 salad chicken breasts (page 242), cut into 5 mm (¼ inch) thick slices, or 4 slices of chashu (page 128)

2 handfuls of mizuna, washed

2 spring onions (scallions), white and light green parts only, finely sliced

4 ramen eggs (page 128), optional

2 nori sheets, cut into squares

8 cherry tomatoes, halved

½ teaspoon yuzu rind, finely chopped (optional)

CHICKEN BROTH

800 g (1 lb 12 oz) chicken bones

400 g (14 oz) pork bones

1 bunch of spring onions (scallions), green bits only

60 ml (¼ cup) sake

FLAVOUR BASE

4 teaspoons yuzu kosho paste

4 teaspoons yuzu juice

8 teaspoons hondashi powder

4 teaspoons salt

SERVES 4, WITH BROTH LEFT OVER

Start by making the chicken broth. Using a knife or scissors, cut the chicken and pork bones into small pieces, if possible, and place in a large stockpot. Cover with 2.5 litres (10 cups) water, add the spring onion greens and bring to the boil.

Once boiling, skim any scum from the surface, then add the sake. Turn the heat down and simmer for 3 hours, skimming off any scum that rises to the surface.

Strain the stock, reserving the liquid and discarding the solids. Pour 1.4 litres (47 fl oz) of the broth into a pot and bring to a simmer. Reserve the remaining liquid for another day.

In a bowl, combine the flavour base ingredients and set aside.

Bring a pot of water to the boil for your noodles. Boil the noodles for 4 minutes, then drain thoroughly.

Turn the heat off under the stock, then whisk in the flavour base mixture. Divide among four bowls, then add the drained noodles.

Top with the chicken or chashu and remaining toppings. Serve piping hot.

PIRIKARA SOMEN

ピリ辛つけそうめん SPICY TSUKE SOMEN

Another popular noodle variation is tsukemen, in which cold noodles are dipped into a strongly flavoured, piping-hot soup, before being slurped. The benefits of this are that the noodles are cooked to the perfect consistency, then chilled, so the diner always has noodles as the restaurant intends, rather than noodles that get soggy and bloated from sitting in the soup too long. Another benefit is that, if the customer prefers a very intense soup, they can drink the soup as it is, but those who prefer a weaker soup can add dashi, usually provided by the establishment, to dilute the soup to their taste.

If you have made the ramen on the previous pages, you can substitute the somen noodles for your ramen noodles, the sliced pork for chashu, and the water for tonkotsu or chicken broth. If you haven't, this is a very easy and tasty tsukemen recipe that'll come together in no time at all.

2 eggs

200 g (7 oz) dried somen noodles

1 tablespoon neutral oil

2 garlic cloves, crushed

1 teaspoon tobanjan

120 g (4½ oz) thinly sliced pork

½ leek, white and light green parts thinly sliced

75 ml (2½ fl oz) mentsuyu (page 216)

1 tablespoon oyster sauce

1 tablespoon sesame oil

1 teaspoon mirin

1 teaspoon rice vinegar

250 ml (1 cup) water

2 spring onions (scallions), white and light green part only, thinly sliced

1 tablespoon grated sesame seeds

SERVES 2

Bring a pot of water to the boil, then carefully drop the eggs in, being careful not to crack them. Boil for 6 minutes, then cool in iced water. Peel and set aside.

Add the somen noodles to the boiling water and cook for 1½ minutes. Pour into a colander and cool under cool running water. Drain thoroughly and place in a serving dish.

Heat the oil in a small saucepan over medium heat. Drop in the garlic and tobanjan and stir for 1 minute, then add the pork and cook until coloured. Add the leek and stir once again for 1 minute.

Stir in the mentsuyu, oyster sauce, sesame oil, mirin, vinegar and water. Bring to the boil, then simmer for another minute, or until the pork is cooked.

Divide between two small bowls and top with the egg. Sprinkle with the spring onion and sesame seeds, then eat by dipping the cold noodles into the broth. After the noodles are finished, you can drink the soup, though if it's too strong for your tastes, you can dilute it with a little water or dashi (page 32).

GYOZA

餃子

A quintessential ramen store side dish, and an item by which many restaurants are judged, gyoza is almost a mandatory order when groups dine out. These crispy bites of juicy minced pork and cabbage are great in between gulps of beer or mouthfuls of hot ramen broth.

Gyoza can come in many shapes and sizes, from tiny bite-sized hitokuchi gyoza (common in tonkotsu ramen restaurants in Kyushu), to monstrously large gyoza as big as a pie. The filling can even come stuffed into a chicken wing. Cabbage and pork are almost universally included; everything else is up to the establishment to decide.

30 gyoza wrappers

1 tablespoon neutral-flavoured oil

1 teaspoon cornflour (cornstarch)

50 ml (1¾ fl oz) water

yuzu kosho, to serve

FILLING

2 tablespoons salt, plus an extra 1 teaspoon

250 g (9 oz) cabbage, finely shredded

250 g (9 oz) minced (ground) pork

100 ml (3½ fl oz) dashi (page 32)

15 g (½ oz) garlic chives, finely chopped

1 cm (½ inch) piece of fresh ginger, peeled and grated

5 shiso leaves, shredded

1 garlic clove, grated

20 g (¾ oz) lard (optional, but recommended)

1 tablespoon soy sauce

1 tablespoon shaoxing rice wine

1 tablespoon cornflour (cornstarch)

½ teaspoon sugar

½ teaspoon ground white pepper

MAKES 30 GYOZA

For the filling, use a gloved hand to massage the 2 tablespoons salt into the shredded cabbage for 2 minutes, until the liquid comes out and the cabbage has softened.

Place the cabbage in a colander and squeeze to extract as much liquid as possible. You should have 140 g (5 oz) of strained cabbage.

Place the cabbage in a large bowl with the remaining filling ingredients, including the remaining teaspoon of salt. Mix together so all the ingredients are incorporated and the dashi has been absorbed.

Divide the mixture among the gyoza wrappers and fold into crescent shapes, one side flat, the other with eight pleats. Place on a tray lined with baking paper, not too close together so they don't stick. (At this point you can freeze them for later, and cook them from frozen.)

To cook the gyoza, heat a small non-stick pan over medium heat (I used an 18 cm/7 inch pan). Add the oil; make sure there is enough to generously coat the bottom of the pan.

Mix the cornflour and water to a smooth slurry and set aside.

Place the gyoza in the pan in a spiral (I could fit eight in my pan comfortably). When you can hear the gyoza sizzling, add the cornstarch slurry, cover the pan and turn the heat to medium–low.

Cook for 6–8 minutes, or when the sound changes from boiling to sizzling, the water evaporates and the bottom is brown. (If using frozen gyoza, this will take 10–12 minutes.) Lift an edge of the gyoza to check if it has browned; if not, cook another minute.

Remove the lid. Place a plate over the pan, then flip the pan and plate so that the bottom of the gyoza is facing up.

Serve with yuzu kosho.

VARIATION: TEBA GYOZA 手羽餃子

Instead of gyoza wrappers, you can stuff deboned chicken wings with the gyoza filling. Debone 30 chicken wings (or have your butcher do this); the mid-part of the wing must not be cut, otherwise the filling will spill out. Marinade the wings in a mixture of 125 ml (½ cup) soy sauce and 125 ml (½ cup) sake for 30 minutes. Stuff the wings with gyoza mixture, then secure each with a toothpick. Brush with the tsukune tare (page 54) if you like, then roast at 180°C (350°F) for 18 minutes, or until the wings are golden brown and the filling is cooked through. Serve with yuzu kosho.

GYOZA PHOTOGRAPHY OVERLEAF →

GYOZA

TEMPURA UDON
天ぷらうどん

The combination of soup and slippery udon noodles with crisp tempura turning slightly soggy from the soup makes this a delicious collection of tastes and textures, with each bite offering something new.

Like making your own ramen noodles, it's worthwhile making fresh udon noodles. It's also possible to break this recipe down into individual components and have them as separate meals. For example, you can make udon noodles and the soup, and have them with some simmered meat and vegetables, or have the tempura simply with rice.

The grated daikon acts as a little palate cleanser between bites of tempura, but it can also be dropped into the soup to add texture and freshness to the udon noodles.

UDON NOODLES

400 g (14 oz) strong flour

2 teaspoons salt

400 ml (14 fl oz) water

rice flour or potato starch, for dusting

Start by making the noodles. In a large bowl, combine the flour and salt. Make a well in the centre, then add one-third of the water and combine. Add another one-third of the water and mix again.

Gradually add the remaining water until the dough comes together and is pliable. You may need more or less water depending on the flour.

Turn out onto a clean bench and knead for 5 minutes, until the dough is smooth, then wrap in plastic wrap and refrigerate for 30 minutes.

Dust the dough with rice flour or potato starch. Using a rolling pin, roll the dough out into a rectangle and slowly keep extending the dough until it is 3 mm (⅛ inch) thick. Wrap and refrigerate again for 30 minutes.

Dust a large cutting board with rice flour. Place the dough on the board and, if it has contracted, roll again to 3 mm (⅛ inch). Dust well with rice flour. Bring the bottom third up to cover the centre, then bring the top third over to cover everything. Dust again liberally and then, using a sharp knife, cut into 3 mm (⅛ inch) wide noodles.

Shake the noodles and dust again if some of them are sticking. Refrigerate until required. (If making the noodles ahead, lay them on a tray, cover tightly with plastic wrap and use within 3 days.)

TEMPURA

100 g (3½ oz) tempura flour, plus extra for dusting

150 ml (5½ fl oz) water

1 egg yolk

600 g (1 lb 5 oz) assorted seafood and vegetables, such as prawns (shrimp), scallops, fish pieces, eggplant (aubergine), capsicum (bell pepper), onion, mushrooms

1 litre (4 cups) neutral-flavoured oil

salt, for seasoning

4 spring onions (scallions), finely sliced

1 lemon, cut into wedges

10 cm (4 inch) piece of daikon, peeled, grated and drained of excess water

NOODLE BROTH

800 ml (29 fl oz) water

160 ml (5½ fl oz) mentsuyu (page 216)

SERVES 4

For the tempura, place the flour, water and egg yolk in the refrigerator to keep as cold as possible before use.

If using prawns, peel and devein them, keeping the tails on. Make three cuts on the underside of each, perpendicular to the tail, then gently crush each prawn, to stop it curling in the fryer.

If using fish, remove any bones and skin, then cut into bite-sized pieces about 1–2 cm (½–¾ inch) thick.

Wash and dry the vegetables, then cut into pieces 1 cm (½ inch) thick, as flat as possible to aid cooking.

Bring a large pot of water to the boil to cook your noodles in, and another pot with the 800 ml (29 fl oz) water for your noodle broth.

In a separate large saucepan, heat the oil to 180ºC (350ºF).

To make the tempura batter, remove the water, flour and egg from the refrigerator. Whisk the egg yolk into the water, then sift in the flour, whisking gently until just incorporated.

Dust your seafood and vegetables with extra tempura flour, using your hands or a brush. Dip them into the tempura batter, then gently lower into the hot oil. Using chopsticks, drizzle a little extra batter onto the pieces to create a more crispy coating. Fry the items for 2–3 minutes, or until a skewer goes through the vegetables easily. The cooking times will be different for each piece of seafood and vegetable, so take some out, cut and taste to see if they are done.

Once done, remove from the oil, drain on paper towel and season with salt.

Boil the noodles for 4 minutes. Meanwhile, divide the mentsuyu among four bowls and add 200 ml (7 fl oz) of the boiling water from the other pot to each.

Drain the noodles thoroughly and place in the bowls. Sprinkle with the spring onion. Place the tempura on side plates and serve with the lemon wedges and a small mound of grated daikon.

Eat the tempura and udon separately, or place the tempura into the soup if you prefer.

TEMPURA UDON PHOTOGRAPHY OVERLEAF →

TEMPURA UDON

CHICKEN CURRY
チキンカレー

The mildly spiced, slightly sweet curry that Japan loves and has nationalised is a meal for any time of the day or night. Families have it with chunks of meat and vegetables as a balanced option, while tradespeople and teenagers have the curry smooth as a sauce for crumbed hunks of pork, deep-fried chicken and seafood or beef croquettes (page 94).

This recipe will provide you with a delicious, simple chicken curry, thick and rich with spice and slowly cooked vegetables. From here you can add more vegetables, as do the families mentioned above, or use it as a sauce for all manner of fried and grilled meats.

5 tablespoons ghee or neutral-flavoured oil

2 onions, sliced

2 teaspoons salt, plus extra to taste

1 garlic clove, grated

1 cm (½ inch) piece of fresh ginger, peeled and grated

1 tomato, diced

1 celery stalk, roughly chopped

½ carrot, roughly chopped

500 ml (2 cups) dashi (page 32) or stock

150 g (5½ oz) potato, peeled and roughly chopped

1 granny smith apple, peeled and diced

4 boneless, skinless chicken thighs, diced into 2 cm (¾ inch) pieces

2 tablespoons honey

2 tablespoons butter

hot cooked rice, to serve

SPICE MIX

1 tablespoon whole cardamom pods

1 teaspoon coriander seeds

1 teaspoon cumin seeds

1 teaspoon black peppercorns

½ teaspoon whole cloves

1 cm (½ inch) piece of cinnamon stick

1 bay leaf

½ teaspoon ground nutmeg

2 tablespoons Japanese curry powder

SERVES 4

For the spice mix, place all the spices, except the nutmeg and Japanese curry powder, in a frying pan. Cook over medium–low heat for about 2–4 minutes, stirring regularly, until fragrant and lightly toasted. Remove from the heat and allow to cool.

Using a spice grinder or mortar and pestle, grind the spice mix to a fine powder – the finer the better. Add the nutmeg and Japanese curry powder, mix well and set aside.

In a large saucepan, heat 3 tablespoons of the ghee or oil over medium heat. Add half the onion and the 2 teaspoons salt and cook slowly until browned. Add the garlic and ginger and cook for 1 minute, then add the spice mix and stir for another minute.

Stir in the tomato, celery and carrot, scraping up any browned bits from the bottom of the pan.

Pour in your dashi and add the potato. Bring to the boil, skim off any foam that rises to the surface, then simmer for 30 minutes.

Add the apple and simmer for another 15 minutes, or until the apple and vegetables are soft. Transfer to a blender and carefully blend until smooth.

Meanwhile, in a clean saucepan, heat the remaining ghee over medium–high heat. Add the chicken, sprinkle with salt and sear until browned on both sides. Remove from the pan. Lower the heat to medium, add the remaining onion and cook for about 15 minutes, stirring regularly, until browned.

Return the chicken to the pan, then add the puréed sauce. Bring to a simmer, then cook for 15 minutes, stirring occasionally.

Turn the heat off, add the honey and butter and stir until combined. Taste and add more salt or honey as desired.

Serve hot, with rice.

KUSHIKATSU

串カツ

The lesser known relative of tempura, kushikatsu are fried morsels of meat, fish or vegetable. The difference is that where tempura is fried in a thin airy batter, kushikatsu is cloaked in a light breadcrumb coating and served on sticks like yakitori. Kushikatsu restaurants can range from cheap and cheerful places in tourist hotspots, perfect for those looking for a quick bite any time of the day or night, to kushikatsu counters where the technique and ingredients are as revered as those in a high-end sushi restaurant. There are even all-you-can-eat kushikatsu restaurants, which provide flour, egg, breadcrumbs and the ingredients for diners to batter and then fry in a deep-fryer set in the centre of the table.

Kutshikatsu restaurants almost always have a deep container of the kushikatsu sauce already at your seat when you arrive. This sauce, similar to a thin, savoury, slightly sour barbecue sauce, remains there all day and night, ready for the next diner to rotate into the seat without the kitchen taking a break between frying loads of freshly crumbed morsels.

Almost anything can be made into kushikatsu, from prawns (shrimp), scallops and abalone to sausages, mochi (rice cakes) and Spam! One rule applies to all kushikatsu restaurants, though: no double dipping!

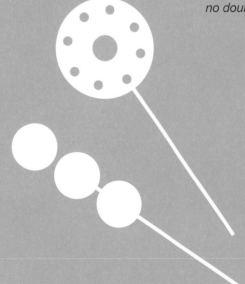

400 g (14 oz) dried panko breadcrumbs

1.5 litres (6 cups) neutral-flavoured oil, for deep-frying

800 g (1 lb 12 oz) selection of meat, seafood and vegetables, cut into small, one-to-two bite pieces; see below for some ideas and combinations

200 g (7 oz) plain (all-purpose) flour

4 eggs, beaten

KUSHIKATSU SAUCE

100 ml (3½ fl oz) water

2 tablespoons oyster sauce

2 tablespoons tonkatsu sauce

1 tablespoon tomato sauce (ketchup)

1 tablespoon soy sauce

1½ tablespoons sugar

SERVES 4

Place all the sauce ingredients in a saucepan and heat, stirring until the sugar has dissolved. Remove from the heat and transfer to a serving bowl; the sauce should be served at room temperature.

To get the authentic crumb texture, use a food processor to lightly blend the panko until it resembles fine breadcrumbs, with no individual crumbs discernible. (The panko for kushikatsu is always much finer than that used for tonkatsu or croquettes.)

Heat the oil to 170°C (340°F) in a large saucepan, ensuring the oil is no more than halfway up the pot, but will be deep enough to completely submerge the ingredients.

Using wooden skewers, or kushi, securely skewer each ingredient separatelty.

Gather three trays or shallow bowls. In the first, place the flour, in the second the beaten egg, and in the third, the panko.

Lightly dust the ingredients in the flour, then dip into the egg and finally into the breadcrumbs. The ingredients should be individually completely coated in an even layer of breadcrumbs, with the skewer totally clean.

Deep-fry the ingredients in batches until cooked – 3–5 minutes, depending on the ingredient and its thickness. As each ingredient is done, drain on a wire rack and keep warm in a low oven.

Serve with the dipping sauce, and a small jar on the side for diners to place their used skewers into.

KUSHIKATSU IDEAS

Meat

· Bacon-wrapped tomatoes
· Bacon, thick cut, layered with onion
· Beef sirloin
· Chicken breast or thigh
· Pork belly
· Frankfurters
· Quail eggs
· Spam

Seafood

· Chikuwa (fish cake)
· Fish fillets
· Oysters
· Prawns (shrimp)
· Scallops
· Squid
· Whole small fish, such as sardines or small mackerel

Vegetable and Dairy

· Asparagus
· Baby corn
· Camembert cheese
· Lotus root
· Mochi (rice cake)
· Onion
· Okra
· Capsicum (bell pepper)
· Pumpkin (winter squash)
· Shiitake mushrooms
· Zucchini (courgettes)

KUSHIKATSU PHOTOGRAPHY OVERLEAF →

KUSHIKATSU

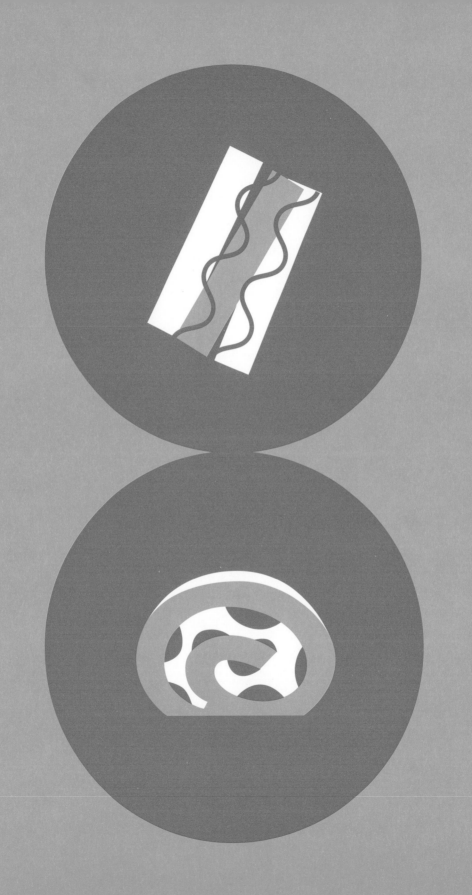

KONBINI

コンビニ

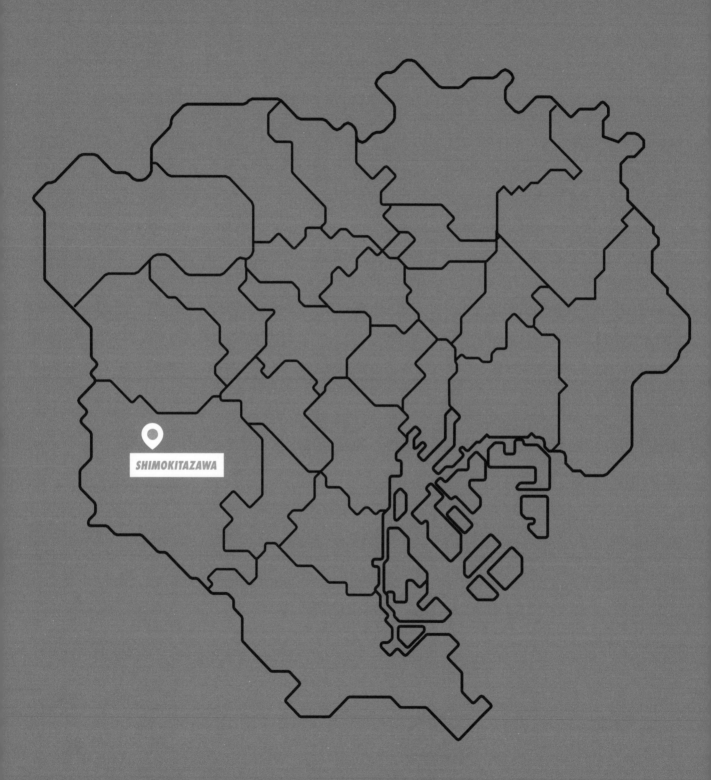
SHIMOKITAZAWA

13:00 *SHIMOKITAZAWA*

A trendy part of Tokyo and considered one of the most desirable places to live, Shimokitazawa is Tokyo's hipster suburb. It's full of vintage and vinyl stores, craft beer pubs and clubs for live jazz bands. The night life, while vibrant, is subdued compared to Roppongi, and therefore it doesn't have the same range of late-night offerings, but being on a main train line makes it a tempting stop on the way home from Shinjuku station.

ポイントカードはお持ちですか？

(Pointo ka-do wa omochi deska?)

Do you have a point card?

The last train has left the station; the streets are now devoid of the besuited salarymen who were so prevalent two hours ago. The only way home now is a taxi … but before hailing one, you see a konbini – convenience store – its eye-catching primary colours and cool white lights calling you in with promises of hot fried chicken, oden and onigiri. One more stop on the journey home.

▶◀● Long the envy of the rest of the world, Japanese convenience stores stock far more than basics. And although other countries are slowly catching up, they still have a long way to go before matching the quality and depth of offerings here. A wall of onigiri and omusubi (rice balls) contain a variety of fillings, such as kombu from the pristine waters of Hokkaido, mentaiko (spicy cod roe) from sunny, coastal Hakata, to umeboshi from mountainous Gunma – next to which is an array of bento boxes and sandwiches, stuffed full of Japanese and Western preparations, like spaghetti and yakisoba, chicken teriyaki and egg salad. The fruit sandwich is particularly popular; an edible artwork of fresh cream, seasonal fruit and soft, fluffy shokupan combine to form a hand-held Victoria sponge cake, ideal for picnics and park benches. ●▶◀ It's not all grab and go. There's a wall dedicated to prepared food in retort pouches for busy home-makers to reheat for a quick family meal. Delights such as buta kakuni (pork belly slowly braised in a sticky soy sauce, page 164), French-style beef stews, Korean kalbi and garlic fried chicken gizzards feature among a multitude of items unique to that convenience store brand. There are also simple items like onsen eggs (page 242), with their yolks and whites set like jelly, slow-poached chicken breast, so tender you could almost cut it with a fork, and thick-cut bacon from the prized Iberico Bellota pork. ▶◀● Wandering around, trying to take in all the options, you will also see a cabinet filled with myriad patisserie items – roll cakes, sweet buns full of sweet azuki and custard, Portuguese-derived castella and an array of choux puffs and éclairs, full to bursting with matcha cream. ●▶◀ Finally, near the cashier lingers the aroma of freshly fried chicken, intermingling with the scent of well-made dashi. With your basket heaving with sandwiches and onigiri,

you might curse yourself for forgetting that some of the best treats are at the counter and struggle with the conundrum of having a finite amount of stomach space and seemly infinite options before you. ▶◀● A cabinet of steaming-hot buns stares down at you. Buns stuffed with enough juicy garlic-scented meat to send vampires running, or a healthier but just as satisfying mushroom and chive bun. Below, there's a fogged-up case that, upon closer inspection, contains dozens of skewers, each holding a long-simmering morsel of fish cake, a succulent piece of chicken thigh or toothsome block of beef tendon in a flavourful dashi stock. ●▶◀ All of which is tempting, but perhaps the most enticing is the fried chicken. In little cardboard containers emblazoned with a kawaii cartoon chicken, each piece is impeccably fried. Uniformly golden, beneath a flurry of spice and seasoning, some chilli, some Southern-style, others lightly scented with lemon, these are the final and most alluring of all the snacks in the konbini.

ONIGIRI

おにぎり

Onigiri is Japan's original convenience food. Rice, packed around a filling (or sometimes plain), makes for a quick, inexpensive and portable meal. Almost anything can be an onigiri filling, so long as it isn't too saucy (like curry) or too hard to chew (like steak).

Onigiri is also a great way to make lunch for the next day. Make extra of some of the fillings listed below, then that evening make onigiri and refrigerate overnight. One of the best ways to enjoy onigiri is to lightly butter a pan and fry the onigiri to create a crisp crust on the exterior, then brush lightly with soy sauce for serving.

600 g (1 lb 5 oz) cooked rice, warm

1 tablespoon rice mix-ins, such as toasted sesame seeds, shio kombu or shirasu (optional)

250 ml (1 cup) water

1 tablespoon salt

fillings of your choice (below)

2 nori sheets, each cut into three rectangles

MAKES 6 ONIGIRI

Mix your rice gently with the mix-ins, if using. Drape a damp, clean cloth over your rice to keep it moist and warm while you shape the onigiri.

Mix together the water and salt and place next to your rice.

With clean hands, dip your hands into the salt water, then divide the rice into six portions. Working with one portion at a time, and keeping the rest covered, flatten one piece and place a tablespoon of your chosen filling in the centre, then encase the filling with the rice.

Press the rice firmly but gently into a circle or triangle, dipping your hands into the salt water if you feel like the rice is sticking to them, then wrap the onigiri in a piece of nori.

Repeat with the remaining ingredients to make six onigiri.

Wrap in plastic wrap, or place in an airtight container and refrigerate for lunch the next day.

FILLINGS

· Buta kakuni (page 164)
· Tuna, mayo & corn – 100 g (3½ oz) tinned tuna mixed with 1 tablespoon mayonnaise, 2 tablespoons cooked corn + ½ teaspoon soy sauce
· Chashu (page 129)
· Cooked salmon
· Gyudon (page 107)

· Katsuobushi
· Mentaiko or tarako
· Mushroom tsukudani (page 96)
· Nikumiso (page 133)
· Sansai (Japanese mountain vegetables)
· Umeboshi, seed removed

BUTA KAKUNI

豚角煮 SLOW-COOKED PORK BELLY

Among the many delights hanging in the chiller of the konbini is always buta kakuni. Pork belly slowly stewed in a sweet, thick, soy-based sauce is a favourite of Tokyo-ites any time of the day or night. The pork stays wonderfully soft even after reheating over the stove or in the microwave, which makes it perfect for making in advance and storing for later.

1 kg (2 lb 3 oz) pork, cut into 2.5 cm (1 inch) thick pieces

6 tablespoons potato starch

1 tablespoon neutral-flavoured oil

1.5 litres (6 cups) dashi (page 32)

3 spring onion (scallion) tops

6 cm (2½ inch) piece of fresh ginger, sliced

135 ml (4½ fl oz) sake

70 ml (2¼ fl oz) mirin

50 g (1¾ oz) zarame or white sugar

50 ml (1¾ fl oz) soy sauce

½ onion, sliced

4 soft-boiled eggs, peeled (optional)

hot English mustard, to serve

SERVES 4

Coat the pork pieces with half the potato starch.

Heat the oil in a frying pan over medium–high heat. Working in batches, sear the pork on all sides until browned evenly, then place on paper towels to drain off the excess oil.

IF USING A PRESSURE COOKER:

Place the pork in a pressure cooker with 750 ml (3 cups) of the dashi, the spring onion tops and half the ginger. Bring up to high pressure and cook for 20 minutes.

After 20 minutes, remove from the heat and leave to cool. When cool, remove the lid and take out the pork, discarding the liquid, spring onion and ginger. Wash the pressure cooker.

Place the pork back into the clean pressure cooker, along with the remaining ginger and dashi. Add the sake, mirin, zarame, soy sauce and onion. Secure the lid on the pot, bring back to pressure and cook for another 20 minutes.

Turn the heat off and let the pressure cooker cool to room temperature. When at room temperature, add the eggs, if using (see note). Place in the refrigerator and leave overnight.

IF NOT USING A PRESSURE COOKER:

Place the pork in a large saucepan and cover with water. Bring to the boil, then empty the pot into a colander, discarding the liquid. Rinse the pork to remove any scum. Place the pork back in the cleaned saucepan with 750 ml (3 cups) of the dashi, the spring onion tops and half the ginger. Bring to the boil, cover with a baking paper cartouche, then simmer over medium–low heat for 1½ hours, or until a knife goes through the pork easily.

Remove the pork from the saucepan, discarding the liquid, spring onion tops and ginger. Place the pork back in the cleaned saucepan with the remaining ginger and dashi. Add the sake, mirin, zarame, soy sauce and onion. Bring to the boil, cover again with a cartouche, then simmer for 60 minutes. Remove from the heat and allow to cool to room temperature. Add the eggs, if using (see note). Place in the refrigerator and leave overnight.

WHEN READY TO SERVE:

Remove the pork and eggs from the pressure cooker or saucepan, leaving the sauce inside. Discard the onion and ginger. Cut the pork into bite-sized pieces. Peel the eggs and cut in half.

Heat the liquid to boiling and reduce by half. Mix the remaining 3 tablespoons potato starch with an equal amount of water, then add it to the pot in a steady stream, stirring constantly. Bring to the boil and cook until thickened.

Turn the heat down to low, then add the pork and eggs. Stir to cover everything in the sauce and allow the pork and eggs to warm through.

Serve individually, or on a sharing plate in the centre of the table, with mustard on the side. It is best accompanied by steamed rice and steamed Asian greens.

NOTE: *For longer storage, do not add the eggs to the sauce. Portion the pork and sauce into heatproof ziplock bags with 1–2 serves per bag and freeze. When ready to eat, bring a pot of water to a simmer and place the bags in the simmering water until warmed through. You can now cook the eggs in the simmering water, peel then add to the hot pork and serve.*

BUTA KAKUNI PHOTOGRAPHY OVERLEAF →

BUTA
KAKUNI

NIKUMAN
肉まん PORK BUNS

These meat-filled delights are so popular in Japan that national chains have started on the back of them. Similar to Chinese savoury steamed buns, the Japanese variety is distinguished by having a juicy minced meat filling heavily scented with onion and served with hot English mustard.

Their aroma is so strong that the Shinkansen bans them from being eaten onboard, and passers-by will give you a wide berth if they see you eating one in public. Late at night, none of this matters, though. What does matter is that they are juicy, delicious, filling and easily reheated, and perfect for picking up from the konbini at 1 a.m.

You can mince or grind your own pork belly for a superior flavour, but for convenience we're using store-bought minced meat for this recipe, enhancing it with bacon and chicken stock powder to help bump up the flavour.

I recommend making double the dough recipe and preparing both the nikuman and vegeman recipe on page 170 at the same time. Both fillings can easily be made in the time the bun dough is resting. Once steamed, the buns can be refrigerated or frozen to be steamed again throughout the week.

mustard, to serve

DOUGH

60 ml (¼ cup) warm water

6 g (¼ oz) dried yeast

60 g (2 oz) sugar

300 g (10½ oz) flour
(see note), sifted

100 ml (3½ fl oz) milk

25 g (1 oz) lard (or vegetable
shortening or oil, for a
vegetarian filling)

FILLING

2 dried shiitake mushrooms,
rehydrated in warm water
until soft, then cut into rough
5 mm (¼ inch) dice

250 g (9 oz) minced (ground)
pork

50 g (1¾ oz) unsmoked
bacon, finely chopped
(optional)

½ onion, very finely
chopped

2.5 cm (1 inch) piece of
fresh ginger, peeled and
grated

1 garlic clove, grated

2 tablespoons soy sauce

1 tablespoon oyster sauce

1 teaspoon sesame oil

1 tablespoon shaoxing
rice wine

½ tablespoon lard

1 teaspoon chicken stock
powder (optional)

½ teaspoon salt

½ teaspoon ground
white pepper

MAKES 8 BUNS

For the dough, add the water, yeast and 1 teaspoon of the sugar to a small jug and mix together. Leave for 15 minutes, or until foamy.

Place the flour in a large bowl. Add the yeast mixture, milk and lard and mix until a smooth dough forms, adding more water if the dough is too stiff. Cover and leave to rest for 1 hour, or until doubled in size.

Meanwhile, line a steamer basket (you may need more than one) with baking paper, punching a few holes in the paper to let the steam through. Mix together all the filling ingredients and set aside.

Knock the air out of the rested dough and divide into eight pieces. Roll each piece of dough into a ball, then flatten into a disc with the palm of your hand. Place one-eighth of the filling in the middle of each dough disc, then envelop the filling with the dough, pinching the dough closed to seal the buns.

Place the buns in the steamer basket/s, leaving a 3 cm (1¼ inch) gap between each other and the walls of the basket if possible, as the buns will expand. Leave to rest for 15 minutes.

Prepare a pot (or two) with boiling water for the steamer basket/s to sit on, then steam for 15 minutes.

Carefully lift the steamer baskets off the pot/s. Remove the buns from the baskets and enjoy with mustard.

NOTE: *Asian grocers usually stock flour specifically made for buns such as these, often labelled as 'bao flour'. If you cannot find it, use plain (all-purpose) flour.*

VEGEMAN
ベジまん VEGIE BUNS

These are a vegetarian variation of nikuman (page 168). While they don't contain any meat, they are just as filling and delectable. The combination of garlic chives and shiitake mushroom, bound with scrambled egg, gives these buns a lovely variance of textures and flavours. It's hard to stop at one.

1 quantity of nikuman dough
(page 169)

soy sauce, to serve

FILLING

1 egg

3 dried shiitake mushrooms,
rehydrated in warm water,
then cut into rough 5 mm
(¼ inch) dice

3 fresh shiitake mushrooms,
cut into 5 mm (¼ inch) dice

100 g (3½ oz) garlic chives,
cut into 2.5 cm (1 inch)
lengths

1 tablespoon roasted
sesame oil

2.5 cm (1 inch) piece
of fresh ginger, peeled
and grated

1 garlic clove, grated

1 tablespoon oyster sauce
or vegetarian oyster sauce

1 tablespoon soy sauce

1 tablespoon shaoxing
rice wine

½ teaspoon salt

½ teaspoon ground
white pepper

MAKES 8 BUNS

Prepare the bun dough as directed on page 169 and let it rest until doubled in size.

Line a steamer basket/s with baking paper, punching a few holes in the paper to let the steam through.

For the filling, heat a dry non-stick frying pan over medium heat. Whisk the egg and pour into the frying pan. Scramble the egg, breaking it up into smaller pieces. When all the egg is set, remove to a small bowl.

Wipe out the pan, then bring back up to medium heat. Add the dried and fresh shiitake and the garlic chives. Stir-fry until the garlic chives are wilted, which should take less than a minute.

Transfer the mixture to a bowl. Add the remaining filling ingredients, including the egg. Mix thoroughly and place in the refrigerator to cool.

When the filling is room temperature or colder, divide the bun dough into eight portions and make the buns as directed on page 169.

Steam for 15 minutes, following the instructions on page 169. Enjoy with soy sauce.

FRIED CHICKEN
フライドチキン

One of the primary ways convenience stores in Japan differentiate themselves is through their fried chicken offering. Each chain's fried chicken is unique, and each has their devotees. Some are small pieces, some are large fillets, some have the bone in, others not.

This recipe is for a large, boneless thigh fillet. For a substantial snack or small hand-held meal, serve in a paper bag for the authentic konbini experience.

4 boneless chicken thighs

250 ml (1 cup) neutral-flavoured oil, approximately

salt and pepper, for sprinkling

SPICE PASTE

1 small knob of fresh ginger, peeled and grated

1 garlic clove, grated

1 tablespoon soy sauce

1 tablespoon sake

1 teaspoon salt

½ teaspoon chicken stock powder

¼ teaspoon ground allspice

¼ teaspoon ground nutmeg

WET COATING

2 eggs

¼ cup (35 g) plain (all-purpose) flour

1 teaspoon chicken stock powder

1 tablespoon soy sauce

1 tablespoon salt

½ teaspoon ground black pepper

DRY COATING

100 g (3½ oz) plain (all-purpose) flour

100 g (3½ oz) potato starch

TO SERVE (OPTIONAL)

shichimi togarashi

mayonnaise

chilli oil

SERVES 4

Check the chicken thighs and remove any bones. Using just the tip of a knife, poke small holes through the meat and skin, to allow the marinade to penetrate all the way into the centre of the meat. Place the chicken between two sheets of plastic wrap and, using a heavy flat object like a meat mallet or frying pan, lightly beat the chicken, concentrating on the thicker sections, to make the thickness uniform.

Mix the spice paste ingredients together in a bowl, then add the chicken. Mix very thoroughly to coat every part of the chicken, then wrap the bowl and refrigerate overnight, or for at least 2 hours.

When ready to cook, remove the chicken from the bowl and pat dry with paper towel to remove the excess liquid, but try not to rub off any of the spice mixture.

Place the wet coating ingredients in a bowl and mix throughly. In a separate bowl, combine the dry coating ingredients. Line a tray with baking paper.

One by one, submerge the chicken thighs into the wet coating, let the excess liquid run off, then coat in the dry coating, pressing the flour into the chicken so that the entire chicken thigh is lightly coated in flour. The chicken should look very evenly coated with the flour mixture with no bare patches. Place on the tray and repeat with the remaining chicken pieces.

Place an oven rack over a tray, ready to drain the fried chicken.

Fill a deep, high-sided frying pan with the oil, to a depth of 2 cm (¾ inch). Over medium heat, bring the oil to 160°C (320°F), or when the end of a wooden chopstick dipped into the oil bubbles lightly.

Add the chicken to the oil, two pieces at a time; the chicken should bubble quickly, but not violently. Cook for 4 minutes on one side, then very carefully turn and cook for 4 minutes on the other side. Check the downward-facing side after 2 minutes to ensure it isn't turning darker than golden brown – if it is, turn the heat down. After the cooking time has elapsed, remove from the pan and drain on the oven rack.

Turn the heat up under the frying pan to bring the oil to 180°C (350°F); the end of the chopstick should bubble more vigorously when dipped into the oil. Working in batches, place the chicken back in and cook for 1 minute each side. After this time, the chicken should be crisp and uniformly golden.

Place on the draining rack and sprinkle with salt and pepper.

Serve hot, with a choice of condiments so diners can customise the fried chicken to their taste.

ODEN

おでん

During winter, one of the great temptations as you near the cash register is the steaming pot of oden. Studded with skewers like a porcupine, the rich broth, which has been bubbling away all day, has absorbed all the flavours of the many sticks of meat, vegetables and seafood that have been luxuriating in it for hours.

The greatest beneficiary of this is the humble daikon. This hockey-puck shaped root vegetable is regarded as the number-one choice in oden for its ability to absorb the many flavours of the simmering broth. Boiled egg is often number two for the same reason.

This recipe is really a set of guidelines for you to build your own oden. Add or remove your likes and dislikes, as if you were the one standing at the konbini register, mulling over how to create the greatest oden bowl ever.

400 g (14 oz) beef tendon
or stewing beef

BROTH BASE

3 litres (12 cups) dashi
(page 32)

250 ml (1 cup) usukuchi
soy sauce

125 ml (½ cup) sake

1 teaspoon salt

2 tablespoons sugar

**SUGGESTED BROTH
ADDITIONS**

4 octopus tentacle ends

½ daikon, peeled, cut into
1.5 cm (½ inch) discs, edges
bevelled and a 5 mm (¼ inch)
cross cut into both sides

250 g (9 oz) konnyaku, cut
into 4 triangles, scored 5 mm
(¼ inch) deep and 5 mm
(¼ inch) apart on both sides

4 eggs

used kombu sheets

CONDIMENTS

mustard

shichimi togarashi

salt

yuzu kosho

miso sauce – combine
2 tablespoons aka miso,
1 tablespoon mirin,
1 tablespoon sake +
1 tablespoon sugar; simmer
until the sugar melts, then
cool

negi sauce – mix together
4 tablespoons sliced spring
onion (scallion) whites +
4 tablespoons mentsuyu
(page 216)

SERVES 4+

Start the recipe 4 hours ahead of eating. Bring a pot of water to the boil, add the beef and boil for 5 minutes. Drain the beef, then rinse to remove any scum.

Place the beef in a clean pot and add the broth base ingredients. Bring to a simmer and cook for 2 hours, skimming off any foam.

Boil the octopus tentacles, daikon and konnyaku for 10 minutes in a separate pot with enough water to cover, then drain and place in the broth with the beef. Simmer together for a further 1 hour.

Meanwhile, prepare the eggs and kombu. Cook the eggs by bringing a pot of water to the boil, carefully dropping in the eggs, then boiling for 8 minutes. Drain and run the eggs under cold water until room temperature. Peel the eggs and refrigerate until required.

Slice the kombu into roughly 10 cm x 1 cm (4 inch x ½ inch) strips and tie each one into a knot. Set aside.

After the beef has simmered for 3 hours, remove it from the pot and cool slightly, then cut into 1.5 cm (½ inch) cubes. Skewer the beef and return to the broth.

Add your eggs and kombu (and any other chosen ingredients) to the pot, arranging them so everything is submerged in the broth, adding more dashi if necessary. Simmer for a further 1 hour over the lowest possible temperature (60–70°C/140–160°F). You can simmer the ingredients for longer at this temperature without detriment.

To serve, divide the ingredients among individual bowls, or place the cooking pot in the centre of the table, with the condiments distributed between diners.

NOTE: *Offering six ingredient additions within the broth should be enough for four people. Besides the ingredients suggested above, other options could include:*

· various fish cakes – no preparation needed

· 250 g (9 oz) atsuage tofu or firm tofu, cut into squares

· 150–200 g (5½–7 oz) boneless chicken thighs, cut into bite-sized pieces, then skewered

· 4 chikuwa, stuffed with enoki mushrooms

· vegetables such as carrot, lotus root, onion, shiitake mushrooms, burdock root, Chinese cabbage (wombok) and tomatoes, cut into bite-sized pieces.

ODEN PHOTOGRAPHY OVERLEAF →

SHOKUPAN
食パン

Every neighbourhood in Tokyo has a small local bakery selling shokupan and common bakery items such as melon pan and cream pan. Items from these places are almost universally high quality and the envy of other countries where loaves are characterless, pre-sliced commodities in an aisle of the supermarket or gas station.

Literally translating as 'bread for eating', shokupan's popularity has skyrocketed in recent years. Fuelled by the interest in 'sandos' – Japanese sandwiches featuring thick cuts of tonkatsu, or salad with soft-boiled egg – popular bakeries can attract long queues and sell out very early. There are also places that specialise in shokupan, using local high-quality flour or dairy from Hokkaido, and blending seasonal flavours such as taro and sweet potato through the bread.

The traditional shokupan is a very light loaf, which has been enriched with milk. It retains the softness of a common white bread loaf, with a touch of richness from the milk and butter. The difficulty is finding balance: the loaf should have a subtle dairy flavour, while also having an ethereal lightness.

220 g (1½ cups) strong flour

165 ml (5½ fl oz) milk

50 g (1¾ oz) sugar

10 g (¼ oz) salt

4 g (⅛ oz) dried yeast

60 g (2 oz) butter, at room temperature, diced

PREFERMENT

220 g (1½ cups) strong flour

165 ml (5½ fl oz) water

2.5 g (⅛ oz) dried yeast

MAKES 1 X 2.8 LITRE (95 FL OZ) LIDDED LOAF TIN

Start by making the preferment. Mix the ingredients together, then cover and leave for 24 hours at room temperature.

The next day, put the preferment in the bowl of a stand mixer. Add all the remaining ingredients except the butter. Knead on low speed using a dough hook for 5 minutes. Scrape down the sides, add the butter and knead for another 10 minutes, or until the dough is very elastic, scraping down the sides of the bowl every 2 minutes.

When the dough is ready, scrape down the sides of the bowl again, then cover and leave to rest in a warm place for 1 hour, or until doubled in size.

Turn the dough out onto a clean bench and divide into three even pieces. Form each piece into a smooth ball, then cover and leave to rest for 20 minutes.

Meanwhile, lightly grease a 2.8 litre (95 fl oz) lidded loaf tin with neutral-flavoured oil.

Lightly flour your bench. Turn one rested dough ball over onto the bench so the smooth side faces down. Using your hands or a rolling pin, stretch the dough to roughly the size of an A4 sheet of paper, or about 20 cm x 30 cm (8 inches x 12 inches). Fold the left side of the dough over two-thirds of the dough. Press down to remove any large air bubbles, then fold the right side all the way over to the left edge.

Take the top of the dough with both hands, then tightly roll from top to bottom to create a log. Seal the excess dough by pinching it together, then place, seal side down, in the loaf tin. Repeat with the remaining two dough balls.

Slide the lid on the loaf tin and leave in a warm place for 1 hour, or until the dough has doubled in size.

When ready to cook, preheat the oven to 180°C (350°F). Bake the bread for 20 minutes, then turn the oven down to 165°C (330°F) and bake for another 15 minutes.

Remove the loaf tin from the oven, carefully remove the lid and turn the loaf out onto a cooling rack. Allow to cool for 30 minutes before slicing.

If using the bread for sando, use it within 2 days. It will be fine as toast for up to 5 days.

SHOKUPAN PHOTOGRAPHY OVERLEAF →

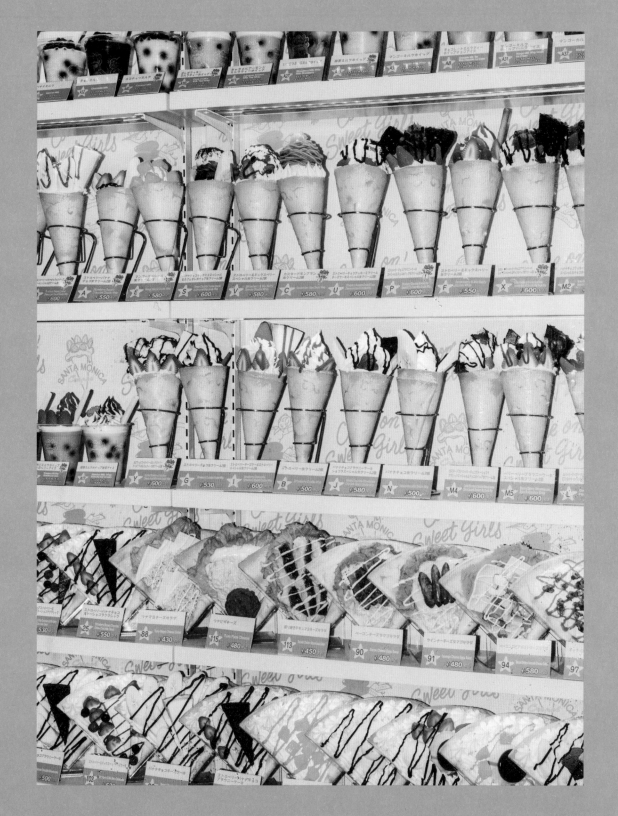

EGG SANDO
タマゴサンド

Japanese konbini have redefined what sandwiches can be. Far from the sad, sloppily assembled examples in convenience stores elsewhere, the sandwiches in Japanese convenience stores are picture-perfect.

They can be as simple as an egg sando, or as over-the-top as a wanpaku sando, filled artfully with an assemblage of ingredients such as eggs, meat and avocado to create a towering meal contained within two slices of bread.

The egg sando is the most famous konbini sando, full of silky mayonnaise and egg yolk, with the slight bounce of the whites providing a textural contrast. Bread and filling in perfect harmony, with a cheeky boiled egg peeking out.

3 eggs

1 tablespoon butter, at room temperature

1 teaspoon Japanese mustard paste

1 tablespoon mayonnaise

½ teaspoon rice vinegar

¼ teaspoon salt

5 grinds of black pepper

2 thick slices of shokupan (page 178)

SERVES 1

Bring a pot of water to the boil, then boil the eggs for 9 minutes. Drain and cool in iced water, then peel and set aside.

In a small bowl, mix together the butter and mustard paste.

Cut two of the eggs in half, then scoop the yolks into a bowl. Add the mayonnaise, mashing the yolks until the mixture is smooth. Add the vinegar, salt and pepper.

Dice the egg whites from the sliced eggs and add to the yolks, mixing well.

Spread the butter mixture on the two slices of bread. Cut the remaining egg in half, then lay the egg halves side by side in the centre of one of the slices. Spoon the mayonnaise mixture over and spread evenly, leaving a 1 cm (½ inch) border at the edge.

Place the other slice of bread on top, buttered side down, then wrap tightly in plastic wrap. You'll be cutting the sandwich into three fingers, so use a marker to draw two vertical lines on the wrap where the halved eggs are, so you can later cut through to reveal the yolks.

Refrigerate for 30 minutes to firm up.

Cutting through the plastic wrap, slice off the crusts, then slice along your marked lines to cut your sando into three fingers. Remove the wrap and serve.

FRUIT SANDO
フルーツサンド

While the egg sando on the previous page may be the most famous konbini sando, the fruit sando may be the next big thing. Fruit sandos showcase the best fruit of the season, encased in a light whipped cream and slices of soft shokupan. A way to accentuate the fruit flavour is by stuffing the shokupan slices with jam. Please experiment with your own fillings and jams to create a spectacular and unique dessert. Slices of mandarin with marmalade, or fresh grapes with grape jelly, or strawberries and red bean paste all make a good starting point.

5 strawberries

2 tablespoons strawberry jam

4 thin slices of shokupan (page 178)

60 g (2 oz) mascarpone

60 ml (¼ cup) whipping cream

20 g (¾ oz) sugar

SERVES 1

Clean the strawberries and cut the tops off. Leave to dry on paper towel in the refrigerator.

Spread the strawberry jam over two slices of the bread, leaving a 1 cm (½ inch) border. Place the remaining slices on top, to make two sandwiches.

Using a pastry cutter or the back of a knife, carefully press firmly just inside the crust, as if you were cutting off the crusts, to seal the two bread slices together, encasing the strawberry jam. Now cut off the crusts, just beyond where you sealed. (If the bread isn't sealed properly, you can pinch it closed with your fingers.)

Using a spatula, massage the mascarpone to soften it.

In a bowl or using an electric mixer, whisk the cream and sugar to soft peaks, then add the mascarpone and whisk to firm peaks.

Lay one of the strawberry sandwiches on a large square of plastic wrap, then spread with a layer of the cream. Place three whole strawberries on the cream in a diagonal line, and a couple in the empty space. Use the remaining cream to fill in the gaps between the strawberries and cover everything in cream.

Place the other strawberry sandwich on top and wrap tightly in plastic wrap. Use a marker to draw where you've placed your line of strawberries.

Refrigerate for at least 3 hours, or overnight.

Keeping the plastic wrap on, cut along the line through the sandwich to divide it in two. Remove the wrap and serve.

MITARASHI DANGO

みたらし団子 MOCHI SKEWERS WITH A SWEET SOY GLAZE

Possibly the most traditional sweet sold in convenience stores, mitarashi dango are glutinous rice balls threaded onto a skewer and coated in a sweet, salty soy sauce. It may sound strange, but it is no stranger than the idea of salted caramel.

Glutinous rice flour provides the chew, while joshinko (Japanese plain rice flour) gives a lightness that is beneficial when the dango cool down, preventing them becoming hard and unpleasant. After boiling and before adding the sauce, the dango can also be grilled, to add a crunchy exterior and lovely caramelised flavour.

DANGO

50 g (1¾ oz) joshinko
rice flour

100 g (3½ oz) glutinous
rice flour

10 g (¼ oz) icing
(confectioners') sugar

150 ml (5½ fl oz) warm water

SAUCE

50 ml (1¾ fl oz) soy sauce

50 ml (1¾ fl oz) mirin

50 g (1¾ oz) sugar

1 tablespoon potato starch

SERVES 5

Bring a pot of water to the boil.

For the dango, mix the flours and sugar in a bowl. Add 100 ml (3½ fl oz) of the water and mix. Gradually add more water, little by little, until it becomes a pliable dough. Divide into 30 balls (dango). Using damp hands, roll each dango in the palms of your hands until smooth.

Working in batches, drop the dango into the boiling water. When they float to the surface, allow to cook for another 2 minutes, before removing and placing in cold water. Repeat with the remaining dango. (The dango can be made up to 6 hours ahead.)

When all the dango have cooled, thread the dango onto skewers (three per skewer) and place on a serving plate.

To make the sauce, place the soy sauce, mirin and sugar in a saucepan. Stir in 100 ml (3½ fl oz) water and cook over medium heat until the sugar has dissolved.

Mix the potato starch with 3 tablespoons water until smooth, then slowly whisk into the sauce. Return to a simmer and cook for about 30–60 seconds, until the sauce has thickened.

Spoon over the dango and enjoy!

ANMITSU

あんみつ MOCHI & RED BEAN PASTE WITH BLACK SUGAR SYRUP

This traditional dessert is wonderful balanced with a mug of hot tea. For the Japanese, it's a taste of nostalgia, a longing for a simpler time – a bygone era of old tea houses and yukata, when the height of luxury was rice, red bean and black Okinawan sugar.

Chewy dango, sweet red beans, cool and wobbly kanten jelly, and a molasses-like black sugar syrup offer up a myriad of tastes and textures that's hard to find outside of Japan.

Below the anmitsu recipe is one for zenzai – a warm red bean soup that's an incredibly simple dessert the following day if you make a double batch of the azuki and dango.

AZUKI

100 g (3½ oz) dried red beans

100 g (3½ oz) sugar

KANTEN JELLY

300 ml (10 fl oz) water

2 g (1/14 oz) kanten agar powder

1 tablespoon sugar

BLACK SUGAR SYRUP (KUROMITSU)

50 g (1¾ oz) kurozato or Japanese black sugar

75 ml (2½ fl oz) water

TO SERVE

½ quantity of dango (page 186), cooked and cooled in cold water (refrigerated if made a day earlier)

seasonal fruit, cut into bite-sized pieces

SERVES 2

For the azuki, put the red beans in a large pot, cover with water and bring to the boil. Once boiling, drain and rinse the beans. Clean the pot, put the azuki back in and refill with fresh water. Boil, then drain again, and repeat one more time. After this third draining, fill the pot with fresh water, bring to the boil, then simmer for about 30 minutes, until the beans are soft.

Drain the beans and clean the pot. Put the beans back in, add the sugar and cook over medium heat for about 5 minutes, until the beans are well glazed in the sugar. Allow to cool, then refrigerate for up to 1 week.

Meanwhile, combine the kanten jelly ingredients in a small saucepan and bring to the boil, stirring constantly. Pour into a square 15 cm (6 inch) tray with high sides. Cool to room temperature, then refrigerate for 2 hours, until cold and set.

For the black sugar syrup, simmer the ingredients in a small saucepan until the sugar has dissolved.

To serve, gently invert the jelly onto a chopping board, then cut into squares. Place into serving bowls. Top with the dango and fruit of your choice, then add a scoop of azuki. Serve the syrup in a small pitcher, for diners to drizzle over as desired.

VARIATION: ZENZAI 善哉

Make one batch of azuki as per the recipe above. Add enough water to loosen the mixture into a soup, then heat to simmering. Add a half-quantity of dango from page 186 (cooked and cooled, but not skewered). Heat the dango in the soup, then divide among bowls and serve. You can add a drizzle of black sugar syrup if desired.

MERON PAN

メロンパン **MELON BREAD**

The West has doughnuts, Japan has melon bread – something everyone remembers from their youth as a grab-and-go pastry. At its most basic, melon bread is a sweet roll covered in a crisp, sugary cap. Sounds simple, but as with all Japanese cooking, focusing on the minute details to make it lighter and tastier is an unending struggle. An open secret, discovered by reading the back of any melon bread wrapper, is that the manufacturers amp up the flavour by adding salted egg yolk to the topping. The cured yolk with a touch of salt brings out a stronger egg yolk flavour, making it feel richer while maintaining the bun's lightness. The name apparently comes from the fact the bun has the appearance of a musk melon. The bun itself does not contain any melon or melon flavouring.

sugar, for coating

BUN DOUGH

150 ml (5½ fl oz) milk

4 g (¼ oz) dried yeast

230 g (8 oz) strong flour

35 g (1¼ oz) honey

25 g (1 oz) butter

4 g (¼ oz) salt

COOKIE DOUGH

30 g (1 oz) butter, at room temperature

75 g (2½ oz) sugar

1 cooked salted egg yolk (optional; see note)

1 egg, whisked

150 g (1 cup) bread flour

MAKES 8

NOTE: *Salted eggs are duck or chicken eggs that have been immersed in a salt brine or encrusted in a salted charcoal paste and left to mature for a month or more. Salted eggs are sold either cooked or raw. If raw, boil in the shell for 15 minutes, then cool under running water. Remove the shell and peel the white away from the yolk. (Chop the white and use in ochazuke, page 220; or zosui, page 103.) Salted eggs are available from Asian grocers.*

Start by making the bun dough. Warm the milk to around 30°C (85°F), either over the stove or by microwaving it for 30 seconds. Mix with the yeast and leave for 10 minutes.

Put the flour, honey and milk mixture in the bowl of a stand mixer. Mix on low speed using a dough hook for 5 minutes. Add the butter and salt and mix for another 10 minutes, or until elastic. (You could also do this by hand, but it'll take longer.)

Place the dough in a greased container, then cover with a lid or plastic wrap. Leave in a warm place – around 40°C (105°F), such as in an oven on very low – for 1 hour, or until doubled in size.

Meanwhile, make the cookie dough. Place the butter and sugar in a mixing bowl. Using a spatula, mix until softened, then add the salted egg yolk and mix well. Add half the whisked egg and combine, followed by the remaining egg. Add the flour and mix using the spatula until all the flour is combined.

Place a sheet of baking paper on the bench. Drop the cookie mixture in the centre, then roll the paper up like a sausage roll to create a cylinder of dough. Place in the refrigerator to harden.

Once the bun dough has doubled in size, turn it out onto the bench and divide into eight. Shape each piece into a round. Cover with a moist towel or plastic wrap and leave to rest on the bench for 20 minutes.

Flatten out each dough ball, then bring the edges back into the centre and seal. This creates layers in the dough and results in a lighter bun. Cover again while you make the cookies.

Line a baking tray with baking paper. Take the cookie dough out of the fridge; it should have hardened by now. Working quickly, so it doesn't soften too much, divide the dough into eight and roll into balls. Place a sheet of plastic wrap on top of each ball and press down with a plate, into even rounds about 5–7 mm (¼ inch) thick.

Place a cookie on top of each dough ball. Wrap the balls, just down to where the cookie dough meets the baking tray, then dip each in sugar, for coating the tops. Use a butter knife to make the distinctive crisscross pattern on the tops. Place the buns on the lined baking tray, leaving a 10 cm (4 inch) gap between them.

Cover again, then leave in a warm spot for about 40 minutes, or until doubled in size.

Preheat the oven to 180°C (350°F). Place the baking tray on the middle rack in the oven and bake for 15 minutes, turning the buns halfway through.

Remove the buns from the oven, allow to cool slightly and enjoy.

The cooled buns can be kept in an airtight container for 4 days. They can be reheated for 10 minutes in a warm oven, or 20 seconds in a microwave.

KASUTADO PAN

カスタードパン CUSTARD BREAD

This custard-filled bun, along with the azuki-filled anpan, are two of the most popular filled breads in bakeries and convenience stores around Japan. The buns are sweet and light, slightly more filling than a melon pan, for times when a more substantial dessert is in order.

1 quantity of melon bread dough (page 190), without the cookie layer

CUSTARD

3 egg yolks

175 ml (6 fl oz) milk

75 ml (2½ fl oz) cream

1 teaspoon vanilla extract

30 g (1 oz) sugar

20 g (¾ oz) cornflour (cornstarch)

65 g (2¼ oz) white chocolate

GLAZE

1 egg

1 tablespoon milk

MAKES 8

Make the melon bread dough as directed on page 191, then leave to rest until the dough has doubled.

Meanwhile, place all the custard ingredients, except the chocolate, in a saucepan and whisk until uniform. Place over medium heat and constantly stir with a spatula, scraping the sides of the pan, until the mixture is very thick (80°C/175°F on a cooking thermometer). Remove from the heat and stir in the chocolate. Transfer to a bowl, press plastic wrap onto the surface of the custard and refrigerate until cold.

Once the dough has doubled in size, divide into eight pieces and roll each into a smooth ball. Cover with plastic wrap and leave to rest for a further 20 minutes.

Remove the custard from the fridge and check that it is room temperature or colder; if not, chilli it a little longer. When the custard is cool enough, divide into eight portions and set aside.

Flatten each dough ball into a circle about 5 mm (¼ inch) thick. Place a portion of the custard in the centre, then fold the dough over into a half-circle. Press the edge to seal.

Using a small knife, cut lines into the sealed part to create a bear paw shape. Place on a baking tray lined with baking paper. Cover and allow to rest again in a warm place for 40 minutes, or until doubled in size.

Preheat the oven to 180°C (350°F).

Mix the glaze ingredients together, then brush over the tops of the buns. Bake for 15 minutes, turning halfway through.

Carefully transfer the buns to a cooling rack and allow to cool for 10 minutes before enjoying.

The buns can be kept in an airtight container for 4 days. They can be reheated for 10 minutes in a warm oven, or 10 seconds in a microwave.

MONT BLANC

モンブラン

This classic French dessert has become almost more synonymous with Japan than its country of origin. Japanese cuisine celebrates the seasons and in autumn, when chestnuts are at their best, crowds gather around famous bakeries and patisseries for their Mont Blanc, featuring gorgeous, perfect candied chestnuts, spaghetti-like strands of chestnut purée and Hokkaido whipped cream. Some stores that specialise in Mont Blanc can be sold out days in advance during peak season.

Those stuck in the office all day can still partake in this modern tradition, as convenience stores will ally with famous chefs and patissiers, for a limited time, to stock their Mont Blanc creations. Here is a simple rendition to enjoy while looking out over falling autumn leaves in front of an open fireplace.

200 g (7 oz) whipping cream

10 g (¼ oz) caster (superfine) sugar

12 cooked chestnuts

150 g (5½ oz) chestnut spread

150 g (5½ oz) chestnut purée

75 ml (2½ fl oz) whipping cream

25 g (1 oz) butter, at room temperature

2 teaspoons rum

ALMOND DACQUOISE

1 egg white (35 g/1¼ oz)

¼ teaspoon cream of tartar

70 g (2½ oz) caster (superfine) sugar

45 g (1½ oz) ground almonds

MAKES 6

Preheat the oven to 160ºC (320ºF). Line a baking tray with greased baking paper. Make a meringue for the almond dacquoise by whipping the egg white with the cream of tartar until slightly foamy, using either a hand whisk or electric beaters. Slowly sprinkle in 20 g (¾ oz) of the caster sugar while whisking, then continue to whisk until the egg white forms stiff peaks.

Mix together the ground almonds and remaining 50 g (1¾ oz) caster sugar, then fold this through the egg white mixture.

Place the mixture in a piping (icing) bag, then pipe six 7 cm (2¾ inch) rounds onto the baking tray, leaving a 2 cm (¾ inch) gap between each round.

Bake for 10 minutes, then remove from the oven to cool.

Whip the cream and caster sugar to medium peaks and place in a piping bag. Pipe a layer of the cream onto the cooled dacquoise, about 1 cm (½ inch) thick, leaving a 1 cm (½ inch) border around the edge. Place a chestnut in the centre. Cover the chestnut with more whipped cream. Repeat until all the dacquoise are covered in cream, then refrigerate.

Mix together the chestnut spread and chestnut purée, then press through a fine-meshed sieve to remove any lumps and make the mixture smoother. Mix in the cream, butter and rum using a spatula until no streaks of butter remain. Place in a piping bag fitted with a Mont Blanc nozzle.

Pipe the chestnut mixture over the chilled cream in a circular motion. A cake turntable is useful for this step, but a good result can be achieved without one. Place a whole chestnut on top.

Cakes can be served immediately or stored in an airtight container in the refrigerator for up to 3 days.

ROLL CAKE
ロールケーキ

Simple in theory, devilishly complex in execution, the perfect roll cake is elusive even for many professional bakers. Something filled with whipped cream has no right being so light and addictive, yet the perfect roll cake is light, easy to eat and pretty as a picture.

This recipe combines the lightest sponge with simple whipped cream to create a classic and mouthwatering roll cake. After you've made it once, you might like to try it again, but add fruit to the centre, or flavour the sponge and cream with various teas and chocolates.

4 eggs

75 g (2½ oz) sugar

40 ml (1½ fl oz) neutral-flavoured oil

65 ml (2¼ fl oz) boiling water

80 g (2¾ oz) cake flour

3 g (¹⁄₁₀ oz) baking powder

FILLING

300 ml (10 fl oz) whipping cream

30 g (1 oz) caster (superfine) sugar

SERVES 6

Preheat the oven to 180°C (350°F). Line a 25 cm x 35 cm (10 inch x 14 inch) roll cake tin or lipped baking tray with baking paper. Grease with baking spray or neutral-flavoured oil.

Separate the egg yolks and egg whites.

Whisk the egg whites with 25 g (1 oz) of the sugar to firm peaks, using either a hand whisk or electric beaters. Place in the refrigerator.

In a separate bowl, whisk the egg yolks and remaining 50 g (1¾ oz) sugar until doubled in volume. Stream in the oil while whisking, then add the boiling water and whisk well. Sift in the flour and baking powder and fold through with a spatula, then fold in the whisked egg white.

Pour into the roll cake tin and smooth the surface. Drop the tin from a height of 10 cm (4 inches) onto the bench to remove any large bubbles, then place into the oven for 12–15 minutes, or until the cake is golden and a skewer inserted into the centre comes out clean.

Remove the cake from the oven. Grease a sheet of baking paper, then place it, greased side-down, on top of the cake and turn it out onto a cooling rack. Allow to cool to room temperature, which will take about 20–30 minutes.

When the cake is cool, make the filling by whipping the cream and sugar to soft peaks.

Remove the top sheet of baking paper from the cake. Spread the cream evenly over the top, leaving a 2 cm (¾ inch) border along one long edge of the cake.

With the side with no cream facing away from you, take the side closest to you and roll it up tightly, using the baking paper to aid you.

Remove the baking paper, then carefully transfer the cake to a serving plate. Cover with an upturned plastic container or bowl so nothing touches the cake. Refrigerate for at least 6 hours, or overnight, to set.

Remove from the fridge, slice and serve.

The roll cake is best eaten the day after making, but will keep for 3 days refrigerated in an airtight container.

STRAWBERRY SHORTCAKE

いちごショートケーキ

Strawberry shortcake is the Japanese celebration cake, used to mark birthdays, anniversaries, special occasions and even Christmas.

Consisting of an almost weightless sponge, whipped cream and perfect strawberries, the shortcake is an expression of lightness and just enough sweetness in a dessert. In convenience stores, it is usually sold in slices, the cross-section showing the carefully assembled layers of cake, cream and fruit. An ideal way to celebrate any little win.

250 g (9 oz) strawberries

250 ml (1 cup) whipping cream

45 g (1½ oz) caster (superfine) sugar

200 g (7 oz) mascarpone

GENOISE SPONGE

3 eggs

1 egg yolk

½ teaspoon vanilla extract

95 g (3¼ oz) sugar

10 g (¼ oz) glucose

30 g (1 oz) butter

35 g (1¼ oz) milk

90 g (3 oz) cake flour

MAKES ONE 15 CM (6 INCH) DIAMETER CAKE

Preheat the oven to 160°C (320°F). Line a 15 cm (6 inch) round cake tin with baking paper.

To make the sponge, place the eggs, egg yolk, vanilla, sugar and glucose in the bowl of a stand mixer.

Bring a pot of water to a simmer and place the stand mixer bowl over the water. Whisk vigorously until the mixture reaches 40°C (105°F), or until it visibly loosens and becomes more watery.

Attach the bowl to your stand mixer. Whisk on high speed for 5 minutes, then on low speed for 2 minutes. The eggs should be very fluffy and smooth.

In a microwave-safe bowl, mix together the butter and milk, then microwave until the butter has melted, about 20 seconds.

Remove the bowl from the stand mixer. Sift in the flour and, using a spatula, fold it through gently, trying not to lose the volume of the eggs. Gently mix in the melted butter mixture.

Pour the batter into your cake tin, then tap the tin on the bench a couple of times to remove large air bubbles.

Bake for 35 minutes, or until a skewer inserted into the cake comes out clean.

Take out of the oven, remove from the cake tin and place on a cooling rack. Allow to come to room temperature, which will take about 1 hour.

Meanwhile, wash the strawberries. Reserve half, preferably the nice-looking ones. Hull the rest and cut nto 5 mm (¼ inch) slices, place on paper towel to absorb the excess water and set aside in the refrigerator.

After the cake has cooled, cut off the browned top and bottom, then cut horizontally through the centre to divide the cake into a top and bottom half.

In a bowl or with an electric mixer, whisk the cream and sugar to soft peaks, then add the mascarpone and whisk to firm peaks. Divide among two bowls, one containing two-thirds of the cream mixture, the other containing the remaining one-third. Place the bowl containing one-third of the whipped cream in the fridge.

Place one half of the cake on a cake decorating stand if available, or on a plate or tray with a low lip. Using the bowl with two-thirds of the cream, spread a 5 mm (¼ inch) layer of cream on the cake. Top with a layer of cut strawberries, then cover completely with a thin layer of cream, another layer of strawberries, then more cream. Place the second cake half on top.

Spread the remaining cream from the same bowl over the top and sides of the cake, creating an even layer, then place in the refrigerator for 1 hour. Don't worry if it doesn't look perfect, we'll cover any imperfections with the cream from the other bowl.

After an hour, coat the cake with half the remaining cream, trying to get it as smooth as possible. Place the remaining cream in a piping (icing) bag fitted with a star nozzle and pipe a border around the top of the cake. Decorate the centre with the reserved strawberries.

Refrigerate again for 4 hours, then serve.

The strawberry shortcake is best eaten within 1 day of being made, but will keep for 3 days refrigerated in an airtight container.

STRAWBERRY SHORTCAKE PHOTOGRAPHY OVERLEAF →

STRAWBERRY SHORTCAKE

BACK HOME

帰宅

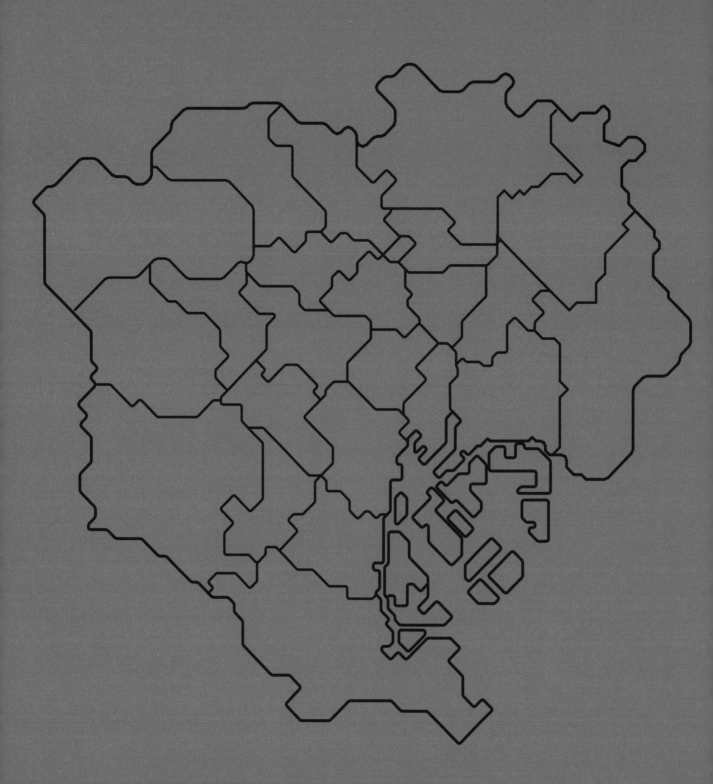

13:30 *HOME*

Legs unsteady from the long, overly warm taxi ride and a parade of whisky highballs earlier, you stagger towards your front door. The taxi moves away quietly behind you, its elderly, spectacled driver squinting as he threads his ageing yet immaculate 1990s Toyota Crown through the dark, narrow lane, back towards the bright city lights.

お帰りなさい

(Okaerinasai)

Welcome home

It's late, but sudden cravings overtake you, and you lurch towards the fridge. The kitchen is suddenly flooded with cool white light. As your eyes adjust, you spot some leftover rice (an accompaniment to last night's curry), half a container of kimchi, a few bacon ends and natto in its distinctive styrofoam squares. You look up at the clock. It's 1.30 a.m. You calculate it'll take 10 minutes to make it, 10 minutes to eat it, 10 minutes to shower before jumping into bed by 2 a.m. More than enough time.

◗◖● With a few Japanese pantry and long-life kitchen staples, it's easy to make a quick and tasty meal in no time at all. The recipes in this chapter are also fantastic ways to use up any surplus rice and ingredients from the preceding chapters, while using as few pots and utensils as possible. And although these recipes are designed to be quick, that doesn't mean they're all empty carbs. You can have a meal full of fresh vegetables and quality protein in a very short amount of time. ●◗◖ Many recipes in this chapter are more like rough guidelines, so feel free to substitute ingredients in and out depending on what you have on hand. Don't have salmon? Use trout or cod. Don't have mushrooms? Use any variety of quick-to-cook vegetables, such as asparagus, capsicum (bell pepper), or zucchini (courgette). ◗◖● A common misconception about Japanese cuisine is that it is very rigid, with lots of unbreakable rules. In traditional kaiseki ryori and sushi, that is true. There are rules such as no sharp points should face the guest, and each kaiseki dish must highlight a particular cooking technique. But in the world of izakaya and late-night cooking, anything goes, as long as it's tasty. The most important rule in Japanese cookery is *mottainai* (勿体無い) – *don't waste anything.* That is always the best rule to follow.

●◗◀ *A NOTE ON SAVING AND REHEATING RICE*

If you have leftover rice, split it into 200 g (7 oz) portions (which is roughly enough for one person), then plastic-wrap them individually in a disc shape, or place in containers and refrigerate for up to 2 days, or freeze for up to 1 month. ◗◀● To reheat, microwave the refrigerated rice for 1 minute, or the frozen rice for 2 minutes. Place in a bowl and gently fluff up the grains and serve. ●◗◀ If you don't have a microwave, you can place the rice in a clean, damp tea towel and steam over boiling water for 10 minutes for refrigerated, or 20 minutes for frozen.

NATTO 101
納豆

'Divisive', 'polarising', 'an acquired taste' – these are a few of the terms most commonly associated with natto outside Japan. These sticky, distinctively flavoured, strongly scented, fermented soy beans are beloved by most Japanese for their taste, convenience and health benefits.

Natto almost always comes in a single-serve styrofoam package with a packet of bonito concentrate and a sachet of mustard. After opening the package, the customary way to eat it is to stir the natto with chopsticks to increase its stickiness. Some say it's best stirred 50 or 100 times, but if you prefer it less sticky, don't stir it at all. You can then add the mustard and natto sauce that comes with it, then pour it over rice. For many busy restaurant workers, natto, rice and a raw egg is the only sustenance they have from morning until the makanai late at night.

A particular trait of Japanese cuisine is matching similar textures, so accompanying natto in the bowl may be okra or tororo (grated sticky Japanese yam), to make a bowl full of sticky goodness.

Natto requires a base carb, such as rice, udon or somen and toppings. Here is a small guide to start you on your natto journey.

BASE

Rice – hot white rice or brown rice

Udon noodles – plain, or with a small amount of broth, such as 100 ml (3½ fl oz) boiling water mixed with 1½ tablespoons mentsuyu (page 216)

Somen – with a small amount of broth (as above)

NATTO

Natto comes in a few styles – large, medium or small bean, and hikiwari (chopped). For beginners, I recommend the hikiwari version, as the stickiness and odour seems diminished when the natto is chopped.

TOPPINGS (1 TABLESPOON PER PERSON)

· Diced avocado
· Sliced spring onion (scallion)
· Shredded shiso
· Chopped pickles
· Sesame seeds
· Onsen eggs (page 242)
· Kimchi
· Okra (blanched and sliced)
· Shredded nori (kizami nori)
· Tororo (Japanese sticky yam)
· Mentaiko
· Diced raw tuna

NATTO KIMCHI CHAHAN

納豆キムチチャーハン NATTO & KIMCHI FRIED RICE

Often natto and kimchi are combined, as the kimchi is said to soften (mask?) the natto's flavour. In this dish, the spicy and sour characteristics of the kimchi balance the nutty funkiness of the natto, which seems to be accentuated by the stir-frying process.

Not a recipe for date night or before an important meeting, but the interesting blend of textures and flavours makes this an enjoyable meal when winding down in front of the TV or lounging on the couch.

A tip I learned for making fried rice, or chahan, using sticky sushi rice, is to massage the grains with mayonnaise to separate them and make the rice easier to stir-fry.

2 tablespoons mayonnaise

400 g (14 oz) cooked rice, cooled

2 tablespoons neutral-flavoured oil

2 eggs, whisked

2 tablespoons chopped bacon, ham or Spam (optional)

4 tablespoons roughly chopped kimchi

2 x 40 g (1½ oz) packets of frozen natto, thawed

1 leek, white part only, very finely chopped

2 teaspoons chicken stock powder

2 tablespoons soy sauce

2 spring onions (scallions), white bits only, finely sliced

Using a gloved hand, massage the mayonnaise into the rice to separate the grains.

Heat a frying pan over medium heat and add 1 tablespoon of the oil. Place a large empty bowl next to the stove, as you will be cooking in batches and adding each batch to the bowl as they are done.

Add the egg to the pan and quickly scramble. When almost fully cooked, remove to the bowl.

Fry the bacon, if using, until browned. Add the rice and fry until lightly toasted, then transfer to the bowl along with the egg.

Pour in the remaining oil, then toss in the kimchi and stir-fry until the liquid has evaporated and the kimchi is slightly charred. Add the natto and fry for another minute, then add the leek and cook a minute further.

Tip the bowl ingredients back in, then add the stock powder and soy sauce and mix thoroughly, Quickly toss the spring onion through to warm it and distribute through the rice.

Transfer to plates and serve.

SERVES 2

WAFU PASTA
和風パスタ JAPANESE-STYLE PASTA

Japanese pasta is very unlike both Italian pasta and Japanese noodles. Richness and umami come not from parmesan, but from butter and a wonderfully versatile Japanese ingredient called mentsuyu.

Traditionally used as a dipping sauce for soba, mentsuyu is a shelf-stable, strongly flavoured liquid you can add to any noodle soup for extra body and flavour. Make some extra to have on hand whenever the mood for noodles takes you.

200 g (7 oz) spaghetti

salt and pepper,
for seasoning

200 g (7 oz) shimeji
mushrooms

200 g (7 oz) enoki
mushrooms

2 tablespoons olive oil

60 g (2 oz) butter, at room
temperature

2 spring onions (scallions),
thinly sliced

4 shiso leaves or a small
handful of parsley, shredded

2 pinches of shredded nori
(kizami nori)

2 lemon wedges

MENTSUYU

40 ml (1½ fl oz) mirin

10 g (¼ oz) sugar

100 ml (3½ fl oz) soy sauce

2 cm (¾ inch) square of
kombu

10 g (¼ oz) katsuobushi

SERVES 2

First, make the mentsuyu. Bring the mirin to the boil in a small saucepan, taking great care as the mirin may catch fire. After boiling for a minute, turn the heat to low and add the sugar. Cook, stirring, until the sugar has dissolved. Add the soy sauce and kombu and bring to a simmer, then add the katsuobushi, pressing down lightly so the katsuobushi is doused in liquid. Simmer on very low heat (it should barely be bubbling) for 5 minutes.

Strain the mixture, reserving the liquid and katsuobushi, pressing down firmly on the katsuobushi to extract as much liquid as possible (see note). This liquid is your mentsuyu.

Bring a pot of water to the boil for your spaghetti. Add a tablespoon of salt, then add the pasta. Boil according to the packet instructions.

Meanwhile, trim the ends off the mushrooms. Tear the shimeji into bite-sized pieces, and cut the enoki in half.

In a frying pan, heat the olive oil and half the butter. Add the mushrooms, season with salt and pepper and stir-fry for a few minutes until wilted. Add the cooked pasta and 100 ml (3½ fl oz) of the pasta water.

Turn the heat off and add the spring onion, remaining butter and 60 ml (¼ cup) of the mentsuyu. Mix well.

Transfer to serving plates, sprinkle with the shiso and nori, and serve with lemon wedges to squeeze over at the last minute.

NOTE: *The katsuobushi can then be dried in a frying pan over medium heat and crushed to use as furikake (rice seasoning). It can also be mixed with sesame seeds and shichimi togarashi and used as a filling or coating for onigiri (page 163).*

You can also save the kombu to use in oden (page 174) and chirashi zushi (page 96).

TAI SAKAMUSHI
鯛酒蒸し SAKE-STEAMED SEA BREAM

An extremely elegant recipe that takes no time at all, this dish relies solely on the quality of your dashi and the freshness of the fish you're using. The tai fillet (Japanese sea bream) will take on a gentle kombu flavour, while releasing its own flavour into the broth, which is then absorbed by the greens and mushrooms.

Your dining companion will think you've spent an age in the kitchen preparing this, but it's only taken 12 minutes and one pan.

375–500 ml (1½–2 cups) dashi (page 32)

1 tablespoon usukuchi soy sauce

1½ tablespoons sake

½ teaspoon salt

2 kombu sheets (slightly smaller than the fish fillets)

2 Chinese cabbage (wombok) leaves

2 handfuls of mixed mushrooms

2 x 200 g (7 oz) white fish fillets, such as sea bream or snapper

2 spring onion (scallion) whites, julienned

2 teaspoons spring onion oil (page 243), optional

SERVES 2

Pour the dashi into a lidded saucepan wide enough to fit both fish fillets side by side, then add the soy sauce, sake, salt and kombu. The liquid in the saucepan should be about 1.5 cm (½ inch) deep; if it's too low, add more dashi.

Place the cabbage and mushrooms in the pan to create a base for the fish to sit on, so the fish will steam above the liquid, rather than in it. Bring to a simmer.

Check the fish fillets and remove any scales and bones. Cut a cross in the centre of the skin about 5 mm (¼ inch) deep, to help the fillets cook more evenly. Sprinkle a little salt on both sides of the fish.

Remove the kombu from the saucepan. Place a fish fillet on each sheet of kombu, then place the fish sitting on the kombu on top of the cabbage. Put the lid on, turn the heat to the lowest possible setting and cook for 8–10 minutes, depending on the thickness of the fish fillets.

Check the fish is done by looking at the centre of the cross. If the fish is opaque and doesn't look raw, remove to a serving plate. If it's still raw, place the lid back on and cook for another minute or two.

To serve, place the vegetables on the side of the fish, garnish with the spring onion and pour the cooking liquid over. Spoon the spring onion oil over, if using, and serve.

OCHAZUKE – A PRIMER

お茶漬け

To call ochazuke simply 'tea over rice' would be doing this dish, which has its origins over 1000 years ago, a great disservice. In a country where every grain of rice is precious, and elaborate tea ceremonies celebrate the tea leaf and its terroir, the combination of these two ingredients is a thing of beauty.

While Japan and its food constantly evolve and change, ochazuke has remained, thankfully, a taste of old Japan. It's very rare to find an ochazuke that has any kind of outside influence. White rice, topped with seafood, sometimes meat, or a single umeboshi, swimming in a tea-based soup or dashi, creates what is possibly the most quintessential mouthful in Japanese cuisine. It's worth seeking out an ochazuke store in Japan as they are often inexpensive and always high quality. Usually they are nondescript stores, hidden in the underground labyrinth of a train station, quickly and efficiently servicing the busy salary workers as they rush to and fro between meetings.

Ochazuke's clean taste and low fat content also provides relief after a night of excessive fried or grilled food and alcohol. It can be the ultimate breakfast the next day as well, and often is for commuters in the early morning.

Below is a brief outline of how to make your own ochazuke using ingredients you like or what's available to you, followed by three recipes to get you started. It may seem like an overwhelming number of options, but as a guide, most ochazuke consists of a base, one primary topping, three or four secondary toppings, and the soup. This is by no means an exhaustive list, so if an idea comes to you that seems like it'll make a good ochazuke, please do try it.

SEE FOLLOWING RECIPES FOR GUIDELINES ON MAKING THE SOUP

Base	Primary topping	Secondary topping	Soup
· Hot cooked rice – either white or brown, plain or onigiri	· Shigureni (shredded braised beef) · Chicken breast · Japanese amberjack (raw) · Japanese sea bream (fresh or kombu cured) · Mentaiko · Salmon (fresh or grilled) · Shirasu (whitebait) · Tempura · Tuna (raw or marinated)	· Arare (rice puffs) · Katsuobushi · Furikake (rice seasonings) · Kinshi tamago (page 96) · Mushroom tsukudani (page 96) · Mitsuba · Nori (sheets or shredded) · Salmon roe · Sesame seeds · Shio kombu (salted kombu) · Shiso (shredded) · Spring onion (scallion), finely sliced · Takana · Tororo kombu (finely shredded kombu) · Vegetables (raw, pickled, steamed or boiled) · Wasabi	· Green tea · Hojicha (roasted) tea · Genmai (roasted rice) tea · Dashi (page 32) · Fish stock

SALMON CHAZUKE

鮭茶漬け

This is the most common ochazuke type in Japan and abroad, and for good reason. The flaky, salty, slightly rich salmon pairs well with the clean, pure flavour of the rice and green tea. Feel free to change the toppings and the soup to suit your tastes.

2 x 100 g (3½ oz) salmon fillet pieces, skin on

300–400 g (10½–14 oz) hot cooked rice

2 spring onions (scallions), white part only, finely sliced

2 tablespoons takana (pickled mustard greens)

2 tablespoons tororo kombu (finely shredded kombu)

2 teaspoons wasabi paste

2 tablespoons shredded nori (kizami nori)

2 teaspoons sesame seeds, ground

SOUP

500 ml (2 cups) green tea (or tea of your choice)

1 handful of katsuobushi (bonito flakes)

2 teaspoons usukuchi soy sauce

2 teaspoons mirin

1 teaspoon salt

SERVES 2

Preheat the oven grill (broiler) to high. Season the salmon fillets on both sides with salt, then place on a greased tray lined with foil, skin side up.

Grill for 8–10 minutes, depending on the thickness of the fillet and how you like your salmon cooked; it should be flaky.

Meanwhile, in a saucepan, heat the green tea to a simmer, then add the katsuobushi and turn the heat off. Leave for 5 minutes, then strain into a clean saucepan. Save the katsuobushi for another use (see note on page 216).

Bring the soup back to a simmer and season with the soy sauce, mirin and salt. Taste and adjust if necessary.

Scoop the rice into serving bowls. Top with the cooked salmon, followed by the remaining ingredients, finishing with the soup.

GOMA TAI CHAZUKE

胡麻鯛茶漬け SESAME & SEA BREAM CHAZUKE

One of the more elegant iterations of ochazuke that is often served in high-class restaurants, this chazuke can be made as shown here, or, if you don't have time, it can be split into many variations. Cure the fish or not, make sesame sauce or omit, make soup from the fish bones or just use dashi (page 32) – it's up to you. The end result will be no less delicious or authentic, simply a variation.

The core of this recipe lies in the freshness of the fish, which is naturally slightly sweet, just warming through on the hot rice, retaining its toothsome texture. The curing process makes the fish more firm and dry, accentuating the texture and flavour.

1 x 150–200 g (5½–7 oz) sea bream or snapper fillet from a 500 g (1 lb 2 oz) fish (save the remaining fillet for another use), skin and centre bloodline removed, bones reserved for the soup (see note)

2 kombu sheets, measuring 20 x 10 cm (8 x 4 inches)

1 teaspoon salt

4 tablespoons freshly ground roasted sesame or sesame paste

2 tablespoons mentsuyu (page 216)

400 g (14 oz) hot cooked rice

2 tablespoons arare (rice puffs)

2 tablespoons shredded nori (kizami nori)

2 teaspoons wasabi

SOUP

fish bones, from above

1 litre (4 cups) water

2 tablespoons sake

3 cm (1¼ inch) square of kombu

2 teaspoons usukuchi soy sauce

2 tablespoons mirin

1 teaspoon salt

SERVES 2

To prepare the soup, place the fish bones in a large saucepan, add the water and bring to the boil. Turn the heat down to a simmer, skim off any foam that appears, then add the sake. Cook for 30 minutes, then strain, discarding the bones. Pour back into a clean saucepan. You should have about 600 ml (20 fl oz) liquid; if you have less, add more water, or some dashi (page 32) if you have it. Add the kombu and bring to a simmer. Season with the soy sauce, mirin and salt. Taste and adjust the seasoning.

While the soup is simmering, prepare the fish by removing any pin bones and scales, then thinly slice, about 3–4 mm (⅛ inch) thick. Wipe the kombu sheets with a damp towel. Sprinkle one piece with half the salt and lay the fish slices on top. Sprinkle with the remaining salt, then cover with the other kombu sheet, pressing lightly to ensure the fish is in contact on both sides. Place in the refrigerator to cure for 30 minutes or up to 1 hour, depending how strong you'd like the kombu flavour.

Make the sesame sauce by mixing the sesame with the mentsuyu, then adding 1–2 tablespoons water until the mixture is the consistency of thick cream.

Once all the elements are ready, assemble the final dish by scooping the rice into your serving bowls and arranging the cured fish on top. Spoon the sesame sauce over and sprinkle with the arare and nori, placing the wasabi on the side.

Serve the soup in a separate vessel so you can enjoy the bowl of rice, fish and sesame sauce on its own, or as a chazuke with the soup poured over.

NOTE: *If you only purchased a fish fillet, ask your fishmonger for about 150 g (5½ oz) of sea bream or snapper bones to make the soup.*

HITSUMABUSHI

櫃まぶし GRILLED EEL CHAZUKE

This Nagoya speciality is a sub-genre of ochazuke, and is often the gateway to an appreciation of freshwater eel, or unagi. The sweet unagi sauce has a smoky flavour and sticky consistency from the grilling of the eel, with its high gelatine content.

Like two courses in one, the best part of hitsumabushi is contrasting the unagi without the soup, enjoying it as you would a donburi (rice bowl), where the strong flavours of soy, wasabi and unagi are at the forefront, before adding the soup and letting the flavours mellow and blend.

Making this dish using raw unagi is very time consuming and requires quite a lot of skill. By using prepared unagi fillets, you can get most of the enjoyment without dealing with slimy eels, and in a fraction of the time.

2 x 250 g (9 oz) prepared unagi fillets (see note)

2 tablespoons sake

2 tablespoons mirin

1 tablespoon zarame or sugar

2 tablespoons soy sauce

400 g (14 oz) cooked rice

2 pinches of ground sansho pepper

2 tablespoons arare (rice puffs)

2 tablespoons mitsuba, roughly chopped

2 tablespoons shredded nori (kizami nori)

2 teaspoons wasabi

SOUP

500 ml (2 cups) dashi (page 32)

1 tablespoon usukuchi soy sauce

1 tablespoon mirin

1 teaspoon salt

SERVES 2

Preheat the oven grill (broiler) to high. Line a grill tray with foil and grease the foil to stop the unagi sticking.

Remove the unagi fillets from their packages, rinse off the sauce and dry with paper towel. (You'll make a better sauce than the one in the bag!)

Cut off and reserve the end 5 cm (2 inch) at the tail of the fillet, and the first 1 cm (½ inch) near the head of the fillet. Place the whole eel fillets, skin side up, on the tray and into the oven.

In a small saucepan, heat the sake and mirin until boiling over high heat. Boil for 1 minute, or until the liquid has reduced by half, then add the zarame, soy sauce and the reserved unagi offcuts. Turn the heat down to medium–high and cook until the sauce has thickened, then turn the heat off. Remove the unagi pieces and discard, or wipe off the excess liquid and feed them to your favourite cat.

For the soup, heat the dashi in a saucepan, then add the soy sauce, mirin and salt. Keep hot.

Check the eel fillets; they should be browned and bubbling. Turn them over so that the flesh side is facing up, then spoon over some of the sauce you just made. Grill for another 3–5 minutes, or until the sauce is bubbling and has reduced to a shiny glaze on the eel. Remove from the oven and spoon some more sauce over. Cut the eel if desired, or leave whole.

To assemble, place the rice in two bowls, spoon on some more of the sauce, then top with the eel. Sprinkle with the sansho pepper, arare, mitsuba and nori, placing the wasabi to the side of the bowl.

Serve the soup in a separate vessel, so you can firstly enjoy the bowl of rice and eel without the soup as an unagi donburi, then add the soup and have it as a chazuke.

NOTE: *Outside of Japan, unagi are usually sold by the fillet, already cooked, covered in sauce, vacuum packed and frozen. It's best to seek out unagi from Japan as it has a firmer, more meaty texture than eel from China.*

HITSUMABUSHI PHOTOGRAPHY OVERLEAF →

YODARE CHICKEN OR TOFU

よだれ/豆腐 MOUTHWATERING CHICKEN OR TOFU

Yodare, or 'mouthwatering chicken', is Chinese in origin, but its simplicity and contrasting tastes and textures has made it very popular in Japan. It is probably slightly milder and sweeter than the progenitor, but feel free to tweak the recipe to suit your tastes.

The list of ingredients may seem long, but most of them are pantry items, and you don't actually need to cook anything if you have the salad chicken ready or are using tofu. To add a carb, you could serve some ramen noodles as a side, hot or cold, or you could add some greens by blanching and chilling some bean sprouts, broccolini or any Asian vegetable and placing it under the chicken to catch that addictive dressing.

2 salad chicken breasts
(page 242), or 300 g
(10½ oz) silken tofu, drained
on paper towel

2 tablespoons very finely
chopped leek, white part
only

2 tablespoons finely
chopped pickled vegetables
(see note)

2 tablespoons roasted
peanuts, pine nuts or
senbei (rice crackers)

2 teaspoons chilli oil, or your
favourite chilli crisp

2 teaspoons spring onion oil
(page 243), optional

1 spring onion (scallion),
green part only, julienned

a pinch of ground sansho
pepper or crushed sichuan
peppercorns

DRESSING

2 tablespoons soy sauce

2 tablespoons black vinegar

2 tablespoons rice vinegar

2 tablespoons roasted
sesame oil

2 teaspoons sugar

2 teaspoons crushed
sesame seeds

2 teaspoons grated
fresh ginger

2 garlic cloves, grated

½ teaspoon ground sansho
pepper or crushed sichuan
peppercorns

SERVES 2

Mix together all the dressing ingredients and set aside.

Cut the chicken or tofu into 1 cm (½ inch) slices and arrange in
serving bowls.

Top with the leek and pickled vegetables, spoon the dressing over,
then finish with the peanuts. Drizzle with the chilli oil and spring onion
oil, if using. Sprinkle with the spring onion and pepper and serve.

NOTE: *Chinese zha cai is the preferred pickle here, but any finely
chopped pickle should provide the flavour and texture contrast you're
looking for. Japanese takana, or mustard greens, work well and can also
be added to any of the ramen dishes in this book, or simply to your next
bowl of instant ramen.*

INSTANT RA-ZOTTO
インスタントラーゾット

Sometimes you want to spend an hour in the kitchen making a feast for yourself and your friends. Other times, you want something quick, but still want a dish with vegetables, substance and taste. Cooking should never be a chore and you should always be able to find a dish that suits your mood and schedule. This recipe takes the fundamentals of risotto – starch cooked in a flavourful liquid – and makes it so simply that the time between opening your fridge and sitting down to eat takes barely longer than the time it takes to boil a pot of water.

I've included the recipe for a lovely risotto alle melanzane (with eggplant), but you can make any risotto recipe you like. Prepare the risotto as usual at the start, but when it comes to the liquid, the rule is to use 220 ml (7½ fl oz) for one packet of ramen.

1 tablespoon olive oil, plus extra to serve

80 g (2¾ oz) eggplant (aubergine), cut into 1 cm (½ inch) cubes

1 tablespoon finely diced onion

1 garlic clove, finely chopped

salt and pepper, for seasoning

1 single-serve packet of instant noodles

½ tomato, diced

50 ml (1¾ fl oz) white wine (optional)

220 ml (7½ fl oz) water or stock (depending on your ramen – see note)

1 tablespoon grated parmesan, plus extra to serve

chilli flakes, for sprinkling (optional)

SERVES 1

For one person, use a 25 cm (10 inch) frying pan; for two people, use a 30 cm (12 inch) pan.

Heat the frying pan over medium heat. Add the olive oil and fry the eggplant for about 5 minutes, stirring now and then, until coloured and cooked through. Add the onion and garlic with a pinch of salt and fry for another few minutes, until the onion has softened.

Meanwhile, crush the instant noodles into 1–2 cm (½–¾ inch) chunks in the packet. Open the packet and remove the flavour pack and oil pack.

Toss the tomato into the pan and fry for a minute. Pour in the wine, if using, and reduce to a glaze.

Stir the crumbled noodles through. Add the water or stock and the contents of the flavour pack (see note). Mix, then spread the noodles out evenly over the base of the pan; they should be covered by about 5 mm (¼ inch) of liquid.

Cook over medium heat for 2 minutes. Taste and check if the noodles are done to your liking; if not, cook for 30 seconds longer.

Turn the heat off and stir in the parmesan and a little ground pepper.

Transfer to your bowl. Serve drizzled with a little more olive oil, with another sprinkling of parmesan and pepper, and chilli flakes if using.

NOTE: *If your ramen is chicken or seafood flavour, you can use half the flavouring pack, and water instead of stock. Some other ramen flavours can be too strong and overpower the other ingredients. If you don't have a chicken or seafood flavoured ramen and you don't have stock, use dashi or water and 1 teaspoon hondashi powder.*

INSTANT CARBONARA

インスタントカルボナーラ

There may be no better way to amplify the flavour of carbonara than this. By using a tonkotsu ramen base, the savoury pork flavour is intensified by the addition of the pork oil and the concentrated tonkotsu seasoning in the ramen. These ingredients are things you will likely have lying around, ready to be made into this dish at any time of the day or night. It's also something to consider the next morning after a big night out. It's basically bacon and eggs, after all.

50 g (1¾ oz) guanciale, speck or bacon, rind removed

1 single-serve packet of instant noodles (preferably tonkotsu flavour)

1 garlic clove, crushed or finely chopped

220 ml (7½ fl oz) water

15 g (½ oz) grated pecorino romano, plus extra to serve

black pepper, to taste

1 egg yolk

SERVES 1

Slice the meat into 5 mm (¼ inch) thick batons.

Heat a frying pan over medium heat. Add the contents of the oil pack from the noodles, then toss the pork in and fry for about 5 minutes, until crisp. Scoop the pork into a bowl, keeping the oil in the pan.

Fry the garlic in the pan for 30 seconds, being careful not to burn it. Add the noodles, water and 1 teaspoon of the tonkotsu flavouring powder from the noodle packet.

Turn the heat up high and boil for 2 minutes, stirring and turning frequently to loosen the noodles and submerge the dry noodles in the liquid.

When the liquid is mostly absorbed, try one of the noodles to see if it's cooked to your liking. When they're done, remove from the heat, add the pecorino and a few grinds of pepper and mix until everything is emulsified. If it seems too dry, add a little more water.

Transfer the pasta to your serving dish, creating a well in the centre. Place the egg yolk in the well. Sprinkle with the crispy meat and extra pecorino, grind a little more pepper over and serve.

POCKY S'MORES

ポッキースモア

Biscuit, chocolate and marshmallow: the delicious flavours of a s'more, rearranged onto a non-traditional kushiyaki.

1 packet of Pocky or equivalent, your favourite flavour

1 bag of marshmallows, your favourite flavour

SERVES 2

Open the packet of Pocky and the bag of marshmallows.

Carefully skewer several marshmallows (depending on their size) onto each Pocky. It may be easier to make a hole in the marshmallows using a skewer before threading them onto the Pocky, as the Pocky are prone to breaking. Do not overload the Pocky, as they may break under the weight of the marshmallows. The marshmallows can also catch fire, so leave enough Pocky to keep a safe distance from your hand and the marshmallows should this occur.

Using your stove, a kitchen blowtorch or, preferably, an open fire, toast the marshmallows, being careful not to burn the marshmallows or yourself.

Allow to cool slightly before devouring.

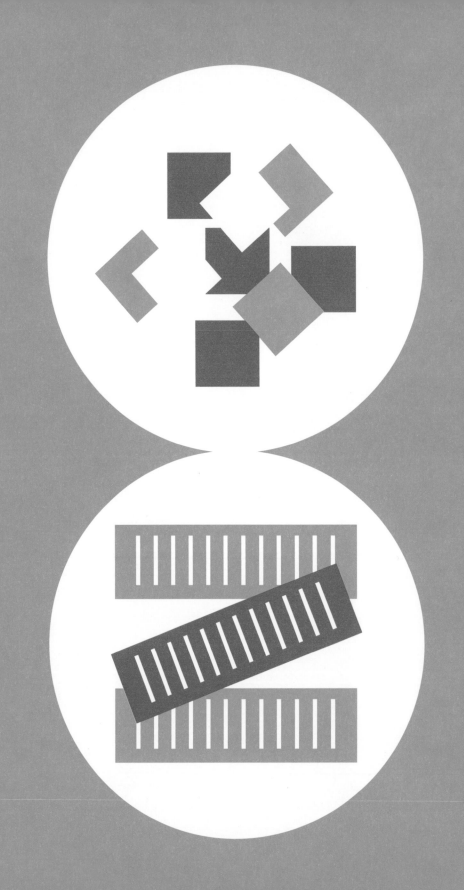

BASICS,
GLOSSARY
& INDEX

ONSEN EGGS 温泉卵

These eggs are traditionally cooked in 60°C (140°F) hot springs, or onsens, where the egg whites set into a jelly-like state while the yolks remain runny, despite being cooked. They are used to top donburi or rice dishes, are added to noodle soups for richness, or used as a dipping sauce for tsukune.

Here is a quick and easy way to cook eggs, with the result very similar to onsen eggs – but without the precise temperature control or timing required for traditional onsen eggs.

2 eggs

SERVES 2

Bring 1 litre (4 cups) water to the boil, then turn off the heat. When the bubbles slow down, carefully, using a slotted spoon, slide the whole eggs into the water. Leave in the water for 11 minutes.

After 11 minutes, remove the eggs. Place in a bowl, then run cold water over the eggs for 1 minute, or until the eggs are no longer hot.

Use immediately, or store in the refrigerator for up to 2 days.

SALAD CHICKEN サラダチキン

A convenience store staple, popular among busy office workers, a simple, well-cooked chicken breast is very versatile. As its name suggests, it is usually used in salads and cold preparations.

2 boneless chicken breasts, approximately 250 g (9 oz) each, skin on or off

2 tablespoons neutral-flavoured oil

2 teaspoons salt

½ teaspoon ground black pepper

6 slices of fresh ginger

2 spring onions (scallions), green part only, cut into 3 cm (1¼ inch) lengths

SERVES 2–4

Place each chicken breast in an individual heatproof ziplock bag, then add half the oil, salt and pepper to each and massage briefly. Divide the ginger and spring onion between the bags, placing them on the underside of each breast, not the smooth side. Seal the bags securely, expelling as much air as possible.

Pour 2 litres (8 cups) water into a large pot with a lid. Turn the heat up to high. While the water heats up, leave the sealed bags containing the chicken on the kitchen counter to come to room temperature.

If you have a cooking thermometer, bring the water to 80°C (175°F), then add the chicken; the chicken will lower the water temperature to around 70°C (160°F). Place the lid on and maintain the temperature of the chicken between 60–70°C (140–160°F) for 40 minutes, before removing the bags from the pot.

If you do not have a thermometer, bring the water to the boil, add the chicken, then turn off the heat and place a lid on. Leave for 40 minutes, then remove the chicken.

Once you have removed the chicken from the water, cool quickly by placing the bags in an ice bath or cold water. Transfer to the refrigerator and use within 3 days.

PONZU ポン酢

An aromatic soy condiment made by infusing soy sauce with Japanese citrus juice, vinegar and bonito flakes, ponzu is often used as a dipping sauce for rich or oily foods, such as beef or tuna tataki and beef hotpot/nabe, as well as in salad dressings.

125 ml (½ cup) soy sauce

125 ml (½ cup) fresh citrus juice (yuzu, lemon, lime, orange or a combination of all), skins retained

35 ml (1¼ fl oz) mirin

20 ml (¾ fl oz) rice vinegar

1 tablespoon katsuobushi

3 cm (1¼ inch) piece of kombu

MAKES ABOUT 300 ML (10 FL OZ)

Combine all the ingredients in a jar, including the citrus skins, ensuring all the solids are immersed in the liquid.

Allow to steep in a dark, cool place overnight, then refrigerate until required. The ponzu tastes best after 1 week, but can be used after 1 day.

After 1 week, strain the ponzu and store in the fridge, where it will keep for up to 3 months.

SPRING ONION OIL ネギオイル

This simple oil brings colour and flavour to many of the recipes in this book, and is a great way to use up any spring onion (scallion) tops you may have in the fridge. This method can basically be used to make an oil out of any herb.

spring onion (scallion) tops

neutral-flavoured oil

Bring a pot of water to the boil, then add the spring onion tops. Cook for about 5–10 seconds, until bright green and slightly wilted, then transfer to a bowl of iced water.

Once the greens are cold, wring out as much water as possible by wrapping them in paper towel and squeezing.

Weigh the spring onions, then measure out twice their weight in oil.

Blend the oil and spring onions together using a blender or small food processor until a bright oil is achieved. Strain the oil through a coffee filter or some muslin (cheesecloth), into a clean jar.

Seal and store in the refrigerator; it will keep for up to 1 week.

GLOSSARY

用語集

Here you'll find a listing of common and less common ingredients you'll encounter in this book, to further your knowledge and understanding of Japanese cuisine.

ABURAAGE TOFU (油揚げ豆腐)

Thin, fried tofu pockets, primarily braised, then used as the casing for inarizushi (tofu pouches stuffed with sushi rice). Aburaage tofu can also be diced and mixed through rice for added flavour and texture.

ARARE RICE PUFFS / BUBU ARARE (ぶぶあられ)

Small, crisp puffs of glutinous rice, sometimes coloured, sometimes plain. Usually used to add crunch to soups and give the liquid a subtle, roasted rice flavour.

ATSUAGE TOFU (厚揚げ豆腐)

A thick block of deep-fried tofu. The fried exterior provides a textural contrast to the soft tofu inside.

BENI SHOGA (紅生姜)

Small shreds of ginger pickled in plum vinegar. Stronger in flavour than gari, it is used in heavy or oily dishes, such as gyudon, takoyaki and yakisoba, to cut through the fat.

BLACK FUNGUS / KIKURAGE (キクラゲ)

Also known as wood ear mushroom, kikurage is a frilly culinary mushroom with a crunchy texture. It is available fresh or dried. If using dried, rehydrate in warm water for 15 minutes before use.

CHIKUWA (ちくわ)

A fish cake that was originally made by being moulded onto a skewer and slowly roasted on a rotisserie to cook. Find it in the freezer section in most Asian grocers.

CHILLI OIL / RA-YU (ラー油)

Japanese chilli oil is often, but not always, milder than Chinese chilli oil. It can use only chilli flakes for flavouring, or can be flavoured with garlic, seafood and spices.

CHINKIANG BLACK VINEGAR (鎮江香酢)

A Chinese vinegar made from fermented black glutinous rice. It is black in colour, mildly acidic, fragrant and complex. If unavailable, substitute Japanese rice vinegar.

DAIKON (大根)

A Japanese long, white radish. It's very versatile and can be used raw, pickled or braised. Raw grated or shredded daikon is a very common palate cleanser in izakayas.

GARI / PICKLED GINGER (ガリ)

Young ginger pickled in a simple rice vinegar, sugar and salt solution. The young ginger naturally turns the solution pink. Some mass-produced gari uses pink food colouring instead.

GLUTINOUS RICE / MOCHIGOME (餅米)

Japanese glutinous rice is naturally sweet and mildly flavoured, equally at home in savoury dishes and sweet. It is sold as whole grains, or ground into a powder (mochiko もち粉), used in sweets.

GOCHUJANG (コチュジャン)

A sweet and spicy Korean fermented chilli paste. Added to dressings, marinades or stir-fries, it adds a nice chilli kick with a lot of depth and complexity.

JAPANESE MAYONNAISE (マヨ)

Japanese mayo is eggier than the Western variety and has the addition of monosodium glutamate to give it a distinctive flavour.

JAPANESE MUSTARD (和がらし)

A very spicy version of mustard, more akin to English than American mustard, used to accompany braised meats, or meat dumplings and buns.

JOSHINKO / JAPANESE RICE FLOUR (上新粉)

Made from powdered short-grain rice, joshinko is less sticky and more mildly flavoured than glutinous rice flour. It is used to give softness and a fine texture to mochi (sweet rice cakes).

KANTEN (寒天)

Also known as agar agar, kanten is derived from an algae and is used to turn liquid into jellies. Kanten can be used as a vegan alternative to gelatine, with the added benefit of staying solid at a much higher temperature (85°C / 185°F as opposed to 35°C / 95°F). Kanten is sold in powdered form or in sticks. I recommend the powdered form as it is easier to use.

KINAKO (きな粉)

A powder made from ground, roasted soy beans, used in many desserts for its nutty flavour.

KONNYAKU (こんにゃく)

Also known as devil's tongue, konnyaku comes in tasteless, jelly-like blocks and is used primarily for its unique texture. High in dietary fibre and very filling, it's often used as a meat substitute in vegetarian cooking.

LYE POWDER (かん水)

Also known as kansui or potassium carbonate, lye powder gives noodles their yellow colour and elasticity. Look for it in Asian grocery stores.

MATCHA POWDER (抹茶)

Finely ground green tea, matcha comes in many grades, from cooking matcha to ceremonial matcha, that is only used in grand tea ceremonies and can cost upwards of $1000 per kilogram. For cooking, use only cooking-grade matcha.

MITSUBA (三つ葉)

Translating as 'three leaf', due to the leaves having three points, mitsuba is a Japanese herb that is added to soups to lend freshness and texture, as the stems retain their integrity after the application of heat. It is also known as Japanese parsley, and is available fresh or dried. There is no need to hydrate it if using dried. Omit if unavailable.

MIZUNA (水菜)

A member of the mustard family, mizuna is a leafy green vegetable that is often used in salads or wilted into stews. It has a peppery flavour and can be found in green and purple varieties.

NIBAN DASHI – SECOND DASHI (二番だし)

Made by re-simmering dashi ingredients a second time in an equal volume of water, niban dashi can be used as a base for stews and simmered dishes such as motsunabe (page 74), fish collar nabe (page 102) and buta kakuni (page 164). Make fresh dashi (page 32) for soups and broths where the dashi flavour is up front, such as miso soup, tai sakamushi (page 219) and ochazuke (page 220).

PANKO BREADCRUMBS (パン粉

Japanese breadcrumbs come in large shards that result in a shatteringly crisp crust on fried products. The dried version is sold in most supermarkets.

SHAOXING RICE WINE (紹興酒)

A Chinese rice wine, used primarily for cooking. Substitute dry sherry or sake if unavailable.

SHIRASU (しらす)

Boiled baby sardines, which are lightly fishy and salty, with a soft texture. Omit if unavailable.

SHISO (しそ)

Also known as perilla leaf, shiso comes in two varieties, a green version called aojiso, and a purple variety called akajiso. The leaves have a distinct, herbaceous flavour, as do the delicate, tiny purple flowers, which are typically eaten with sashimi. Shiso can be found fresh in Asian greengrocers in the refrigerated section.

SOMEN (そうめん)

A thin wheat noodle that is most often served cold, with a flavourful sauce alongside for dipping.

TENMENJAN (甜麺醤)

A soy bean–based sauce that has a sweet, rich flavour. Substitute with hoisin sauce if unavailable.

TOBANJAN (豆板醤)

Made from broad beans, and also known as doubanjiang, this chilli sauce is most famously the flavouring for mapo tofu. Its salty, savoury, spicy flavour is also the basis for many Sichuan and Japanese–Chinese dishes.

TONKATSU SAUCE (とんかつソース)

Japan's answer to barbecue sauce is a blend of spices, fruit, vegetables, ketchup and worcestershire sauce. It is very versatile and can be used as the flavouring for yakisoba, on top of okonomiyaki, and as a sauce for fried food – including, of course, tonkatsu (fried pork cutlet).

TORORO KONBU (とろろ昆布)

Konbu that has been very finely shaved into hair-thin ribbons. It is used to top salads and tataki, and is added to soups to contribute a salty, umami flavour.

WAKAME (若布)

A type of edible seaweed that is usually sold dried, to be rehydrated and added to soups and salads for texture.

INDEX

THANK YOU

Thank you to Smith Street Books for giving me the opportunity once again to share my stories and recipes with you.

Thank you to my editor Katri Hilden, book designer Michelle Mackintosh, Japanese photography team led by Gorta Yuuki, my small band of recipe testers, and Caryn. I am also ever appreciative of the team at Minamishima restaurant for allowing me the time to write this book and supporting me along the way.

Published in 2022 by Smith Street Books
Naarm | Melbourne | Australia
smithstreetbooks.com

ISBN: 978-1-922417-59-6

Publisher: Paul McNally
Editor: Katri Hilden
Design and Illustration: Michelle Mackintosh
Typesetter: Heather Menzies, Studio31 Graphics
Food photographer: Gorta Yuuki
Food stylist: Yuko Yamaguchi
Food preparation: Naoko Akanuma and Yoshiko Yamase
Proofreader: Ariana Klepac
Indexer: Helena Holmgren

Printed & bound in China by C&C Offset Printing Co., Ltd.

Book 199
10 9 8 7 6 5 4 3 2 1